Euripides: Ion

DUCKWORTH COMPANIONS
TO GREEK AND ROMAN TRAGEDY

Series editor: Thomas Harrison

Aeschylus: Agamemnon
Barbara Goward

Aeschylus: Persians
David Rosenbloom

Aeschylus: Seven Against Thebes
Isabelle Torrance

Euripides: Bacchae
Sophie Mills

Euripides: Heracles
Emma Griffiths

Euripides: Hippolytus
Sophie Mills

Euripides: Ion
Laura Swift

Euripides: Iphigenia at Aulis
Pantelis Michelakis

Euripides: Medea
William Allan

Euripides: Phoenician Women
Thalia Papadopoulou

Seneca: Phaedra
Roland Mayer

Seneca: Thyestes
P.J. Davis

Sophocles: Ajax
Jon Hesk

Sophocles: Electra
Michael Lloyd

Sophocles: Philoctetes
Hanna M. Roisman

Sophocles: Women of Trachis
Brad Levett

DUCKWORTH COMPANIONS
TO GREEK AND ROMAN TRAGEDY

Euripides: Ion

Laura Swift

Duckworth

First published in 2008 by
Gerald Duckworth & Co. Ltd.
90-93 Cowcross Street, London EC1M 6BF
Tel: 020 7490 7300
Fax: 020 7490 0080
inquiries@duckworth-publishers.co.uk
www.ducknet.co.uk

A catalogue record for this book is available
from the British Library

ISBN 978 07156 37449

Typeset by e-type, Liverpool
Printed and bound in Great Britain by
CPI Antony Rowe, Chippenham, Wiltshire

Contents

for Russell

Acknowledgements

This book was written while I held a Junior Research Fellowship at Trinity College, Oxford, and I would like to thank the college for its generous support during this time. I am also grateful to Deborah Blake, Tom Harrison and the anonymous reader at Duckworth for their helpful advice. Thanks are also due to Bill Allan, Melanie Marshall, and David Wallace for their comments on the book and proof-reading of earlier drafts.

1

Play and Myth

Ion is not one of Euripides' best known plays, but it is one of his most appealing. The plot takes a commonplace of religious myth (the rape of a young girl by a god) and gives it an ironic twist, applying the values of the contemporary world to the heroic past.[1] *Ion* is the story of a boy's journey to adulthood, and a mother's search for her lost child, but the play also explores ideas about family, religion, identity and knowledge, and despite its playful tone, these themes are handled in a serious and thought-provoking way.

This chapter aims to introduce the reader to the play through a discussion of the Ion myth, its treatment by Euripides, and its pre-history and development in Greek and later literature. The chapter begins with a summary of *Ion*'s plot, and then explores our evidence for other versions of the myth within the Greek tradition. By recognising where Euripides differs from previous versions, we can gain insight into the original audience's expectations and the dramatic significance of the innovations Euripides makes. The last part of the chapter will discuss the afterlife of the Ion story, and the play's reception in the post-classical period. Here too, observing changes in how the myth is handled not only illuminates later generations' approaches to *Ion*, but can also help us to assess the themes and priorities of Euripides' own version.

The plot of *Ion*

Like all Greek tragedies, *Ion* is structured around the alternation of spoken dialogue between the actors (episodes), and songs performed by the Chorus (stasima). Yet despite this apparently simple sequence, *Ion* stands out for the elegance of its structure. Despite being set within a time-period of only a few hours, the play represents the whole of Ion's life, and both his past and his future are essential to understanding the significance of what we see on stage. Within the action, Euripides sets up a complex pattern of scenes which echo or mirror each other, encouraging his audience to draw links between what they have seen. We must therefore look in more detail at the shaping and organisation of the individual scenes and songs. (For explanations of technical terms, see the Glossary on pp. 121-2.)

1-81: prologue
The play begins with a prologue spoken by Hermes. He narrates the circumstances of Ion's birth: Apollo raped an Athenian princess, Creousa; she subsequently concealed the pregnancy and exposed the baby, but Apollo arranged for him to be brought to Delphi and raised at his temple. Creousa is now married to a non-Athenian, Xouthos, who provided Athens with military aid during a recent war. However, the couple are childless, and are coming to Delphi to seek advice from the oracle. He finishes by explaining that it is now Apollo's plan to integrate Ion into Xouthos' household, and prophesies his future as the founder of the Ionian Greeks.

82-183: Ion's monody
Ion enters with a group of temple attendants, and sings a solo outlining his duties as a servant of Apollo, and expressing his joy at serving the god.

184-236: choral *parodos* (or entry song)

The Chorus, handmaidens of Creousa, enter and admire the
artistic marvels of the temple. Ion and the Chorus then sing a
brief lyric interchange, where he explains the religious rules
which must govern their behaviour in the sanctuary.

237-451: first episode

(237-391: Ion, Creousa and Chorus)
Creousa enters and begins a conversation with Ion, who is
struck by her sad demeanour. We see an immediate bond
between them, as Ion pities Creousa for her childlessness, and
she pities him for his lack of a mother. Creousa is moved by Ion's
story to ask for his advice in finding out her own child's fate, but
to avoid the shame of disclosing her story pretends the events
happened to a friend of hers. Ion's response, however, is to
advise her not to question Apollo, claiming that the god will
punish any who reveal a story which presents him in a bad light.

(392-451: with Xouthos too)
Xouthos arrives, having visited the nearby oracle of Trophonius
to get a preliminary response, and been told that he and
Creousa will not leave Delphi childless. He instructs Creousa to
decorate the altars with laurel, while he enters the temple to
consult the oracle. Ion, left alone on stage, attempts to go back
to his tasks, but is distracted by his concern about Apollo's
behaviour in the story Creousa has told him. He condemns the
gods for acting as the arbiters of a set of morals for mortals
which they themselves do not abide by, and urges Apollo to use
his power to pursue good.

452-509: first stasimon

The Chorus sing a short ode, praising Athene, the patron goddess
of Athens, and calling upon her and Artemis to bring Creousa's
prayers to pass. This then leads them to further reflection on

the importance of children to human happiness: children, they say, are better than wealth or power. Their train of thought moves on to imagine the girl from Creousa's story abandoning her baby. They claim that children born to the gods from mortal women are a source of unhappiness and bad luck.

510-675: second episode

(510-65: trochaic tetrameters, Ion and Xouthos)

Ion enters, shortly before Xouthos returns from the shrine, having been told that the first person he meets as he leaves the temple will be his son. The dialogue which follows creates a humorous tone, contrasting Xouthos' enthusiastic embraces with Ion's horror at this strange behaviour. Ion eventually accepts that Xouthos must be his father, and asks who his mother is: a question Xouthos is unable to answer. Raking over Xouthos' past life, they eventually conclude that Ion must have been conceived when Xouthos attended the Bacchic mysteries in Delphi.

(566-675: iambic trimeters)

Xouthos instructs Ion to accompany him to Athens as the heir to the throne. Ion, however, is reluctant and presents several objections. He fears a cold welcome from the Athenians as the bastard child of a foreign father. He also anticipates a hostile response from Creousa, whose pain at her childlessness will be heightened by Ion's arrival. Finally, he rejects the life of a king, claiming that he prefers his simple life at the shrine to the fear and hatred that surrounds power. Xouthos brushes away Ion's concerns. He does, however, decide to wait until Ion has arrived in Athens before publicly acknowledging him as his son, in order to find a suitable opportunity to persuade Creousa to accept him. In the meantime, he announces a banquet to be held in Ion's honour, and warns the Chorus not to tell Creousa about Ion's paternity, on pain of death.

676-724: second stasimon

Both characters leave the stage, and the Chorus sings another ode, commenting on the events they have just witnessed. They anticipate Creousa's pain at the news, and express concern about Apollo's motives. Their grief on Creousa's behalf springs partly from their loyalty to her. However, as the ode develops, their hostility to the news also takes a nationalistic turn, as they express resentment at Xouthos, a foreigner, taking over the throne of Athens, and importing Ion, a non-Athenian heir.

725-1047: third episode

(725-62: Creousa, Old Man, Chorus)
Creousa enters, accompanied by her old slave, and asks the Chorus what Xouthos has learnt from the oracle. The Chorus tell her that she will never have a child.

(763-99: kommos: Creousa singing in lyric, Chorus and Old Man speaking in iambics)
The Chorus tell the distraught Creousa about Apollo's gift of a son to Xouthos. Creousa and the slave ask about the details of what has happened.

(800-58: iambics)
The slave suggests that the situation has been set up by Xouthos, to create a plausible way of introducing his bastard son into Creousa's household and to oust Creousa herself. He encourages Creousa to turn her distress to vengeance and goads her on to kill Ion and Xouthos, offering to do the deed himself. The Chorus also swear their loyalty and complicity in the murder.

(859-922: Creousa's monody)
In her distress, Creousa now reveals the truth about her rape by Apollo and her subsequent abandonment of the baby. She curses Apollo and his neglect of their son.

(923-1047: iambics)

The slave is shocked to learn Creousa's story. He first suggests burning Apollo's temple down, then proposes killing Xouthos, but eventually both he and Creousa agree that Ion is her true enemy, and they decide to assassinate him using a poison she inherited from her grandfather. Creousa asks the slave to wait until Ion reaches Athens, but he points out that this will make it more likely that she will be suspected; instead they decide to kill him straight away, at the celebration Xouthos is arranging.

1048-1105: third stasimon

The Chorus sing an ode invoking Hecate, goddess of witchcraft, and asking for her help in fulfilling Creousa's plans. Again, they stress the ignominy of Creousa's position, and also the shame to the city as a whole if Athens is ruled by a foreigner. The ode ends with an attack on men and the double standards applied to men and women: popular tradition holds women to be sexually unfaithful, but in fact Xouthos' example shows that men are guilty of far greater infidelity.

1106-1228: fourth episode

A Messenger enters, looking for Creousa. Her plot has been discovered and her life is in danger. The Messenger describes Xouthos' banquet in detail, before narrating the assassination attempt using poisoned wine. Ion received the cup, but when a sudden hush fell, he recognised it as a bad omen, and poured his wine on the ground. One of the sacred doves then drank the wine and was killed by the poison. Under torture, the slave revealed his part in the plan, and Creousa has now been condemned to death.

1229-49: fourth choral ode (in place of stasimon)

(1229-43: anapaests; 1243-9: astrophic lyric)

Horrified, the Chorus sing a response fearing for their own lives as well as Creousa's.

1250-1622: *exodos*

(1250-60: trochaic tetrameters, Creousa and Chorus)
Creousa reappears, fleeing an angry crowd, and takes refuge at the altar. By the laws of Greek religion, a suppliant at an altar cannot be touched.

(1261-1438: Ion, Creousa, Priestess)
Ion enters, and finding Creousa at the altar, rails against the injustice of her claiming sanctuary in Apollo's name. He and Creousa exchange furious words. The quarrel, however, is interrupted by the Priestess, who enters from the shrine and tells Ion to put aside his anger and go to Athens to seek his mother. To assist him, she has brought the items which were left in his cradle as a baby. Creousa recognises the cradle and leaves the altar to greet Ion with joy. Ion is initially incredulous, and assumes Creousa is trying to trick him, but when she is able to identify and describe the items in the cradle, he acknowledges her as his mother.

(1439-1509: lyric interchange)
Ion and Creousa express their joy at their reunion, with Creousa singing in lyrics, while Ion continues to speak in iambics. Creousa tells Ion the story of his birth.

(1510-end: Ion, Creousa, Athene)
Ion still doubts Creousa's claim that Apollo is his father and resolves to go into the temple to ask the god himself. As he attempts to enter, Athene appears on the *mêchanê,* explaining that she has been sent by Apollo, who does not want to confront the mortal characters in case they blame him for his past behaviour. Athene reveals Apollo's role in events, and prophesies Ion's future role in founding the Ionian Greek cities and establishing their links to Athens. She ends by instructing Creousa and Ion not to tell Xouthos the truth about Ion's paternity, so

that he will continue to accept him as his son. The play ends with Creousa's retraction of her earlier curses against Apollo as the characters joyfully leave for Athens.

The myth and its development

Greek tragedy draws on a rich and complex mythological world for its plot-lines. The stories and characters are not invented by the dramatist, but drawn from the world of myth, which was familiar to the audience from a variety of sources ranging from earlier poetry to sculpture and vase-painting. While the broad outline of the myth is known to the audience, the poet has a large degree of flexibility in how he chooses to tell his version. Sometimes this means that the same characters are presented differently in different plays. For example, we find Odysseus presented as a clever diplomat (Sophocles' *Ajax*), or as a slippery manipulator (Euripides' *Iphigeneia at Aulis*); Electra as an innocent young girl (Aeschylus' *Libation Bearers*), or as a vengeful and powerful figure (Sophocles' *Electra*). Alternatively, the details of the plot itself can change. Thus, in Euripides' version of *Medea*, Medea herself deliberately kills her children, rather than it being done by others or being a mistake; in Euripides' *Helen*, Helen is not the guilty adulteress of the usual tradition, but an innocent victim who never went to Troy. Thus the existence of a well known set of stories and characters could be used as a platform from which to innovate, rather than a stifling set of 'rules'.

The myth of Ion is a relatively obscure one in the Greek tradition; however, we find several references to a figure named Ion as founding father of the Ionian Greeks. A fragment of Hesiod refers to the three sons of Hellen: Xouthos, Dorus and Aeolus (the latter two the founders of the Dorian and Aeolian Greeks). Herodotus names Ion as the son of Xouthos, and says that he is founder of the Ionians. Herodotus also incorporates the idea of a connection between Ion and Athens: in his account Ion was a military leader of the Athenians, and the four tribes of Athens were named after his sons. We find a more detailed account of Ion's genealogy in Pausanias (writing in the second century AD), where he is said to be the son of Xouthos (an exile from Thessaly) and a daughter of Erechtheus, and to have had a brother called Achaeus. According to Pausanias, after Erechtheus' death, Xouthos was asked to decide which of his sons should succeed him; he chose the eldest, Cecrops, and as a result was banished from Athens by the other sons. After Xouthos' death, his two sons became rulers of Ionia and Thessaly (Achaea) respectively. Ion maintained his links with Athens, however, and was buried in Attica, having died leading the Athenians in war.[2] From its earliest appearance, then, the Ion myth is used as a genealogical explanation of Greek ethnic identity.

We also know that Sophocles produced a play based on the Ion myth, and it is often thought that his version, like Euripides', made Apollo Ion's father (cf. Soph. frr. 319-22 Radt). Since we do not know whether Sophocles' play was written before or after Euripides', it is unclear which poet was responsible for creating the story of Ion's divine birth. It is, however, significant that this innovation was probably made by an Athenian poet, since Ion's divine descent glorifies the Ionians above the other Greek tribes. The existence of a cult of Apollo Patroos ('ancestral Apollo') also suggests the existence of a tradition that made Apollo part of Athenian heritage.[3]

The tradition of the Ion myth casts light on Euripides' version of the myth in various regards. It firstly tells us that Ion's Athenian connection was well-established, and that the idea of a racial and political connection between Athenians and Ionians pre-dated the fifth century. However, Ion's tie to Athens is strengthened by making him the son of Apollo rather than Xouthos, as it removes any non-Athenian connection. Ion is no longer half-Athenian (and merely on his mother's side); his only mortal heritage is that of the Athenian royal family. Athene's prophecy that Xouthos and Creousa will give birth to sons called Dorus and Achaeus makes the Athenian royal house the ancestor of the other Greek tribes, and therefore the most important (1589-94). Ion is glorified by being the son of a god, and by implication so are the Ionian people, whose divine descent is contrasted with the mortal origins of the Dorians and Achaeans. Ion's divine birth, and the mystery of his parentage, also facilitates other aspects of the play, such as the motif of mistaken identity (see pp. 69-71).

Afterlife

Compared to many Greek tragedies, *Ion* has enjoyed relatively little reception in later drama or other art forms.[4] *Ion* was a relatively obscure myth even in antiquity. Euripides' *Ion* is mentioned by Demetrius, a rhetorician writing around the first century BC, in his *On Style* (195), so we know that the play was still being performed at this time. However, it was not one of the myths reworked by Ovid, or restaged by Seneca. The Ion myth's absence from Latin poetry (and also from Aristotle) no doubt hampered its transmission into the Renaissance period, since most of the Greek plays which became popular were known to later readers by one of these routes. There are various factors which may explain this. The preference for tragedies with unhappy endings, following Aristotle, meant that lighter plays such as *Ion* tended to be overlooked, or regarded as lightweight and inferior companions to darker and more serious works. The Athenian theme also makes *Ion* a less transferable play than many: the aetiological nature of the plot may have obscured the themes of the play which are of more universal interest, while to later generations the patriotic tone is at best irrelevant, and at worst distasteful. In addition, the play's rather ambiguous presentation of Apollo is often felt to be problematic, as later interpreters feel a conflict between the depiction of the god as a callous rapist and the play's optimistic ending. Indeed, in 1692, an influential edition of the *Poetics*, published by Dacier, claimed that *Ion* would never succeed on stage.[5]

The first English version of *Ion* was a play by William Whitehead, entitled *Creusa, Queen of Athens*, and was first performed in 1754 in London.[6] Whitehead's version removes the supernatural and divine elements from Euripides' play: Ion is the product of a clandestine marriage between Creusa and a (low-born) Athenian called Nicander, who is exiled from Athens by Creusa's angry father. Creusa is then married to Xuthus: none her family know that she was married to Nicander rather than simply having an illegitimate relationship, while Creusa herself believes Nicander to be dead. However, Nicander in fact survives and, calling himself Aletes, raises Ion at the temple. The play thus revolves around the reunion of Ion's parents as much as the boy's own search for his identity. Creusa and Nicander are reunited, but die at the end of the play: Creusa drinks the poison meant for Ion, in shame at her own bigamy, while Nicander takes a wound meant for Ion. Ion is left an orphan, but has learnt his true identity and his claim to the throne of Athens. The play was a success, and was put on seven times in the next five years. Its popularity was partly related to the way it engaged with issues of contemporary concern, discussed extensively by Hall and Macintosh in their recent book on Greek tragedy in the British theatre.[7]

The population increase of the early eighteenth century had led to a greater number of unwanted births; the first Foundling Hospital had been established by an Act of Parliament in 1740, after considerable debate. The hospital was controversial because it was widely believed that institutionalising adoption would encourage immorality, and that a child had to be brought up in its birth-family in order to become a well-adjusted adult.

The Ion myth thus takes on a new relevance, as the play presents Ion as a likeable and intelligent young man, despite his inauspicious start in life. In addition, the play was performed in the year after the Marriage Act was passed in Parliament. This legislation tightened the regulations surrounding marriage, and clamped down on common-law and clandestine marriages, which had previously counted as valid. The play's presentation of Creusa and Nicander's affair as a clandestine marriage rather than an illicit affair is important. The play affirms the new political *status quo*, and presents the lovers as victims of the inadequate laws of their time which allowed Creusa to commit bigamy.

Further stage adaptations of *Ion* appeared during the nineteenth century, including a German version by Schlegel in 1803, directed by Goethe, which met with a cold reception.[8] However, a more popular version of the myth appeared in 1836, by Thomas Talfourd. Talfourd's *Ion* is only loosely based on Euripides' version. The play is set in Argos rather than Athens: probably a deliberate attempt to avoid the political associations of Athens, which was already by the nineteenth century being used to debate contemporary ideas about democracy. In the play, Argos is ruled by a tyrannical king, and suffering from a plague. Ion, an orphan brought up by a priest of Apollo, discovers he is the king's son, and thus heir to the throne. However, he learns of a prophecy that the city will only be freed from the plague when the king's line is destroyed. In a noble spirit of altruism, Ion commits suicide, and founds a republic. As Hall and Macintosh note, Talfourd's play is deeply political.[9] The play was produced only a few years after the Reform Act of 1832, which doubled the size of the electorate. As such, the play's portrayal of the virtuous Ion, who empowers the people of Argos, compared to the wicked tyrant who crushes them, is thoroughly supportive of the Whig policies of the time. Talfourd's version of *Ion* was tremendously successful, and its republican message meant that it became particularly popular in the USA.

Both Whitehead and Talfourd's versions of *Ion* suppress the play's religious element, and restructure the plot in such a way as to remove any need for a god. This discomfort with the fantastic elements of Greek tragedy is reflected in classical scholarship of the time. In 1890, the classicist A.W. Verrall produced a new translation of Euripides' *Ion*, which attempted to rationalise the plot. The play was influenced by a translation which had appeared the previous year by one H.B.L.; this took a similarly rationalistic line, suggesting that Creousa had been raped by a mortal man, and taken him to be Apollo because his blond hair shone in the sun. Verrall's own interpretation also seeks to make sense of the plot while removing the divine elements. He suggests that Ion is the son of Xouthos, conceived in the circumstances Xouthos describes (550-4), while Creousa's baby (the product of her rape by a 'ruffian') really did die when she exposed it. The encounter between Ion and Xouthos was arranged by the authorities at Delphi, who are trying to reunite the boy with his father, and these same authorities get together fictitious 'clues' to persuade the desperate Creousa that Ion is really her son. Rationalising the plot in this way requires significant ingenuity, as well as reinterpreting the most natural way of reading Euripides' play. Verrall's motivation to do this derived from his view of Euripides as a rationalist, who put gods on stage only to discredit traditional religion.[10] Victorians used the term 'rationalist' to describe anti-clericals: hence Euripides' engagement with intellectual issues became conflated, in contemporary eyes, with an attack on organised religion (see Chapter 3 for Euripides' presentation of the gods).[11]

In the twentieth century, the appeal of *Ion* has revolved more around psychology and characterisation. A particularly powerful twentieth-century interpretation is that of the poet

H.D. (Hilda Doolittle). H.D.'s *Ion* was begun in 1934, and was written while the poet was undergoing sessions of psycho-analysis with Freud. The poem is a translation of virtually all the play, but it suppresses the political, sophistic, or patriotic elements. For example, her translation omits Ion's speech to Xouthos about the perils of kingship, and Athene's prophecy of the future of the Ionian race. Similarly, the poem downplays the ethical crisis around Apollo's behaviour: while Ion's criticism of Apollo is translated, it is severely compressed, and is easily overlooked by the reader. Thus, the play focuses firstly on the mystical and ritual aspects of *Ion*, and secondly on the charac-terisation of Ion and Kreousa (H.D.'s spelling), and the relationship between them.[12] In her commentary on the play, H.D. criticises 'rationalist' interpretations of Euripides such as that of Verrall, and describes Ion's monody as a 'vibrant super-abundance of ecstasy before a miracle'. Her translation of the monody captures the religious flavour of the original with its short lines and repetitive language, which give the speech a ritualistic tone. H.D. is interested in capturing what she calls the 'psychic affinity' between Ion and Kreousa, especially in their initial dialogue. While she translates the sense of the interchange, each line is vastly compressed into a few syllables. Ion and Kreousa speak in incomplete sentences, picking up on each other's language, and finishing each other's sentences. The result is the sense of a melding of the two characters, a sense of uncertainty as to where either of them begins or ends. As well as an exploration of human relationships, H.D.'s *Ion* is also an allegory for the human journey of self-discovery and knowledge, signified by H.D.'s description of Athene as intellect personified. The patriotic triumphalism of Euripides' play is thus transformed into a more general and humanistic victory.

Interest in *Ion* has continued into more recent times, and Euripides' play was reperformed several times in the late twen-tieth and early twenty-first centuries. Most recently, Lydia

Koniordou's *Swallow Song* (a translation of excerpts from Greek tragedy with a theme of parenthood) and Colin Teevan's *Seven Pomegranate Seeds* (myths involving the separation of mother and child) include the Ion-Creousa story.[13] The twenty-first century has also seen a new opera of *Ion*, by the Indian composer Param Vir. The opera is closely based on Euripides' play, with a libretto by David Lan, and the first full production opened to rather mixed reviews in 2003.[14]

We can see, then, that *Ion*, like all Greek tragedies, can be adapted to reflect the preoccupations of successive generations. The play's attractive characters and varied moods make it well equipped to do so, for *Ion* can be made more or less humorous, political, feminist, or philosophical, depending on the adaptor's own demands. To understand Euripides' own treatment of these themes, however, we must assess the play in the light of its social and historical contexts, and it is to these that we shall turn in the following chapter.

2

Tragedy and its Contexts

Greek tragedy deals with themes of universal interest, hence modern directors continue to stage it more than two thousand years after it was originally composed. However, in interpreting these texts it is important to read them in the light of the culture that produced them. The performance context of ancient drama was very different to that of the modern theatre, and while many elements of the plays still resonate with us today, others are tied into the preoccupations of a society alien to our own. This chapter will therefore set *Ion* in the cultural and historical contexts of fifth-century Athens, discussing both the immediate context of its performance and wider political or social issues relevant to the themes of the play. In addition, the form and style of Greek tragedy was governed by traditions different to those of modern drama, but with which Euripides' audience would have been familiar. The final section of this chapter will therefore examine the conventions of ancient tragedy, and discuss how Euripides manipulates these for dramatic effect.

The City Dionysia

Like most surviving Greek tragedies, *Ion* would have been first performed at the Athenian festival of the City Dionysia (also known as the Great Dionysia).[1] The Dionysia was one of the most important festivals of the Athenian year, and an opportunity to display the city's poetic and musical talent. The tragedy performances took the form of a competition between three poets, each of whom was allocated a day on which to put on a production of three tragedies and a satyr play (a more light-hearted play featuring a chorus of satyrs: mythological creatures associated with Dionysus and famous for drinking and debauchery). While tragedy formed the central part of the Dionysia, it was not the only type of poetic performance at the festival. Before the tragedy competition came a competition in dithyramb (a choral song in honour of Dionysus performed by fifty singers), held between the ten tribes of Athens. Each tribe entered one chorus of adult men, and one of boys. After the tragedy, the festival ended with a comedy competition, where five poets each entered one play. As well as the poetry perfor-mances, the festival also included a vast procession through the city in honour of Dionysus, sacrifices of bullocks, and large-scale public feasting.

Tragedy was therefore part of a large public festival, and the function of each play was a competitive one, for each poet's aim was to win the prize. At its core, tragedy is therefore best under-stood as a genre which aimed at popular appeal. This does not, however, imply that tragedy was aimed at the lowest common denominator: Aristophanes' comedy *Frogs* contains jokes which show that the Athenians prided themselves on the sophistica-tion of their understanding of the plays.[2] In any case, the audience would have been composed of Athenians from different social classes, and it was therefore important to please the educated elite (who were responsible for funding the plays) as well as poorer citizens.[3]

As well as spectacle and competition, the Great Dionysia provided a forum for showcasing Athenian poetic and musical talent to a wider audience. The festival was held in late March, by which time the seas were navigable once more and interna-tional travel was possible. The Dionysia was widely attended by foreigners and in particular by those from other cities in Athens' empire. To understand the relevance of this to the festival, and to *Ion*, we must look briefly at how the empire developed, and the mechanisms that Athens used to assert her control of it.

Athens and her empire

In 478, the Greek cities had successfully beaten off two waves of Persian attacks. However, it was far from clear that the Persian threat was over, especially for the Eastern Greek cities, located on the fringes of the Persian empire. In 477, a new League was formed for those cities which wished to continue fighting the Persians. Its treasury (and therefore headquarters) were located on the island of Delos, but Athens took on the responsibility of leadership.[4] Over the next few decades, the Delian League became an Athenian empire, as Athens exerted increasingly tight political and economic control over its allies. In 454 the treasury moved from Delos to Athens, thus establishing Athens' economic control of the League's wealth. Garrisons were frequently placed in allied cities, as well as Athenian administrative controllers, and law-suits of a serious nature were transferred to Athens. The language used to describe the League became increasingly proprietorial: cities began to swear loyalty to Athens rather than to the allies, and some Assembly decrees from *c.* 445 refer to the allies as 'the cities which the Athenians control'.[5] The tribute paid by the allies funded the Athenian navy, thus ensuring the continuity of Athens' power over her allies: when a city revolted from the League, Athens' military strength could easily bring it back in line.

To maintain control over the empire, Athens made use of cultural and ideological tools as well as military and financial ones. For example, Athens tended to support democracies in her subject cities, and Thucydides' account of the revolt of Mytilene in 427 suggests that the Athenians relied on the support of the democratic factions within the cities.[6] It is in this light that we should understand the importance of Athens' Ionian identity. The allied cities were predominantly Ionian Greeks, in particular the island cities of the East Aegean. Thus, by emphasising a shared ethnic identity, Athens could claim more justification for the empire.[7] We see a similar manipulation of ethnicity in Thucydides' description of Athenian involvement in Sicily, where Athens' shared Ionian links with Leontini are used as a pretext to justify military intervention against the Sicilian Dorian cities.[8] Athens' Ionian heritage became increasingly prevalent in art and culture during the sixth and fifth centuries: for example, Ionian architectural features on Athenian public buildings are often believed to have been an ethnic statement.[9]

We see similar use of cultural activities for political purposes in the City Dionysia. After the foundation of the Delian League, the Dionysia became the occasion for the allies to pay their tribute to Athens. The tribute was exhibited in the theatre, thus explicitly linking Athens' imperial power and her cultural achievements. This message was also strengthened by the other rituals which preceded the tragedy performance. The first was a ceremony to honour the sons of men who had died fighting for Athens: the boys who had reached adulthood that year were paraded in front of the audience, presented with a suit of armour at public expense, and given prestigious front-row seats. The second ceremony involved honouring those who had benefited the city (both citizens and foreigners). The Dionysia was therefore used to convey a strong civic message, emphasising Athens' benevolence as well as her power and wealth, and the loyalty felt to her by both citizens and allies. The Dionysia indicates the value placed on fulfilling one's civic duty, and also highlights how Athens constructed an image as the natural leader of her empire.[10]

We can see, therefore, that the festival at which tragedy was performed contained strongly patriotic elements. This should alert us to the civic role that public poetry performed, which in turn informs our reading of the parts of *Ion* that deal with Athens. *Ion* acts as an Atheno-Ionian foundation myth, explaining Athens' links with Ionia, and suggesting an Athenian right to control Ionia. Ion, an Athenian by birth, is destined to found and rule the Ionian cities; Athene prophesies that these cities will provide strength to Athens (1584-5), thus establishing the empire as divinely ordained. Similarly, *Ion* is designed to please the islanders in the audience as well as the Athenians, for Ion's divine parentage suggests that the Ionians are superior to other Greek ethnicities (see further pp. 78-80).

Dating the play

Euripides' career as a playwright spans the second half of the fifth century, and coincides with that of Sophocles. Euripides first entered the tragedy competition in 455, coming third (i.e. last), and continued writing plays until his death in 407/6. Of the twenty-two entries for the Dionysia he produced, only four were awarded first prize (compared to Sophocles' total of eighteen victories).[11] This statistic is often used to back up the belief that Euripides' plays were considered shocking and subversive by the Athenian audience. However, it is important to remember that only three poets were given the opportunity to participate in the festival each year, so the fact that Euripides was regularly given a slot suggests strong support for his work in Athens.[12]

As with many Greek tragedies, we have no concrete evidence for the date of *Ion*. In order to date the play, some scholars try to relate it to external events and to look for contemporary allusions. However, this kind of allusion in tragedy is (if present at all) extremely veiled, which makes this way of dating the play subjective.[13] For example, a recent study of *Ion* by Katerina Zacharia argues that the play's focus on the theme of empire suggests that it was written after Athens' defeat in Sicily in 416, which led to concerns that the empire might fragment, and hence a desire to strengthen patriotic loyalty among the allies.[14] However, one could equally well suggest that before the Sicilian disaster Athens was enjoying a period of optimism (reflected in the play), and that the attempt to invade Sicily demonstrated the kind of confident imperialism evident at the end of *Ion*. Similarly, Zacharia argues that the play cannot post-date 412, because she believes the references to the four tribes of Athens would evoke the Oligarchic Coup of 411, and contain negative political overtones. However, any attempt to guess how the audience would respond to these references (both before and after 411) is pure speculation: if we found solid evidence that *Ion* was produced after the Oligarchic Coup, we would no doubt find new interpretations of the play's political and nationalistic stance. Tragedy rarely engages with direct contemporary events except on the most generic level: the issues which it raises are widely applicable, and defy being pinpointed in time. The play's pro-Athenian stance and imperial theme would be relevant to any moment in the fifth century, and attempting to date it any more precisely relies on our own presumptions rather than any evidence provided by the play itself.

Attempting to establish the date of a play by internal criteria is also problematic. For example, it might be tempting to assume that Euripides' *Alcestis* and *Helen* were close in date because of their similarities in tone and style, but we know from external sources that the two plays were written more than twenty-five years apart (438 and 412 respectively). While many of the lighter plays of Euripides do indeed date to the later period of his career, *Alcestis*, his earliest surviving play, suggests that we should be wary of attributing a systematic development or change in mood. In addition, the fact that we have only seventeen tragedies of the 92 plays attributed to Euripides should make us cautious of any attempt to generalise.[15]

However, we do have one reliable method for dating Euripides' plays, which is his handling of metre. Over the course of Euripides' career, he increases the number of trisyllabic feet ('resolution') in his iambic trimeters: thus, by comparing a given play to others which are metrically similar, we can give it a rough date (see the appendix for an explanation of these metrical terms).[16] This evidence suggests that *Ion* was composed in about the middle of Euripides' career, at around the same time as *Trojan Women* (415). We can thus say with reasonable confidence that *Ion* was composed at some time in the period 420-410, and we can further say that it is likely to have been composed towards the middle or later part of this period.[17] However, any attempt to suggest a more precise dating relies on criteria which are too subjective to be secure.

Formal features and structure

The basic structure of Greek tragedy is the alternation of spoken episodes performed by actors and choral odes involving singing and dancing. However, this distinction between actors and chorus is not absolute: actors can also sing, and often do so at moments of great emotion (such as Creousa's disclosure of her rape, 859-922), while the Chorus Leader frequently joins in the dialogue to comment on a particular character's viewpoint, or to contribute to the development of the plot (for example she tells Creousa about Apollo's oracle to Xouthos at 774-5, and advises her to take refuge at the altar at 1255-61).

By Euripides' time, the number of actors allowed in a tragedy was fixed at three, though the poet could also include an unlimited number of silent parts, for dramatic and visual effect. The actors were professionals, paid by the state. As drama developed over the course of the fifth century, it became increasingly professionalised: actors set themselves up in troupes, and each troupe operated its own internal hierarchy, with the star parts reserved for the top actor ('protagonist').[18] The three actors divided the parts between themselves, and it is possible to ascertain which actor played which part by working out which characters are on stage simultaneously. In *Ion*, for example, the actor who plays Xouthos must also play the Priestess, since both characters are on stage with Ion and Creousa.[19]

In addition, each tragedy contained a chorus of fifteen, consisting of ordinary citizens recruited from the Athenian populace.[20] For a modern audience, accustomed to a plot- and action-focussed type of drama, understanding the purpose of the tragic chorus is particularly challenging. In a sense, the Chorus has a dual identity. On the one hand, it represents a set of characters in the play (in this case female attendants of Creousa); these women express their opinion, take sides, and are implicated in the events of the play. The Chorus has only limited ability to take part in the action, but can nevertheless influence events: in *Ion*, the Chorus' decision to disobey Xouthos and reveal his adoption of Ion sets in motion Creousa's murder attempt (760-2, 774-5). On the other hand, the Chorus emerges from a legacy of group song and dance. Choral performance formed a central part of Greek festive and religious life, long predating tragedy; indeed, many modern scholars believe that tragedy developed from these performances.[21] As such, the tragic Chorus has an important identity as a Chorus *per se*, not simply as a group of characters in the play. The Chorus' odes draw on a tradition of choral song, which often contained a didactic and moralising tone. The Chorus therefore acts as a bridge between the world of the drama and the world of the audience, guiding our interpretation of the play, and helping us to see how the events on stage fit into a broader understanding of the world.

In terms of stagecraft, choral odes can be used to account for the passage of time: for example, the third stasimon (1048-1105) is meant to represent the time taken for the preparation of Xouthos' feast, the murder attempt, and the discovery of the plot. In practical terms, choral odes also give the actors time to change their costumes between scenes. However, choral odes in fifth-century tragedy are never simply interludes, but are intended to contribute to the audience's understanding of the play, and enhance the development of its themes.[22] In *Ion*, the Chorus constantly use their odes to comment on the action, and by doing so are able to influence the audience's perspective. The Chorus' loyalty to Creousa throughout the play encourages us to see her as a sympathetic character, as well as providing her with a friendly confidante. The Chorus' freedom to generalise and moralise also allows them to draw on traditional ideas and myths to bring out the broader themes of the play. For example, their statement in the first stasimon that having children is better than possessing wealth or power (485-7) draws on a poetic convention of assessing and ranking desirable things; putting children first thus highlights the importance of parenthood in the play.[23]

A Greek audience would also anticipate certain conventional features in the action of the play: for example a messenger speech; a formal debate between two characters (*agôn*); a divine appearance (*deus ex machina*). The stylised nature of Greek drama can be off-putting to a modern reader, and it can be easy to perceive these formal devices as a straitjacket for the poet. On closer analysis of the plays, however, we see the tragedians draw on these conventions and on their audience's expectations to enhance the dramatic effects of their works, and *Ion* is no exception.

For example, Euripides frequently opens his plays with a prologue by a single character, setting out the 'story so far', and ensuring that the audience knows which of many possible versions of the myth the poet is using. In *Ion*, as in several other plays, the prologue is given by a god, who has knowledge of the future hidden from the mortal characters.[24] However, Hermes' prophetic powers turn out to be fallible. As his predictions of Ion's smooth integration into Xouthos' household unravel, we become increasingly unsure whether the god's plan can be enacted. The contrast between Hermes' confident announcement of the divine plan (69-75) and the chaos which the mortal characters make of it adds to the sense of uncertainty about the gods which the play creates.

Similarly, many of Euripides' plays include an *agôn* scene: a set debate between two characters, usually consisting of two opposing speeches (roughly equal in length), followed by alternating lines of dialogue (*stichomythia*). These scenes allow the poet to showcase his rhetorical skill, and to explore key issues and moral cruces of the play from opposing viewpoints. In *Ion*, we anticipate an *agôn* in the scene between Ion and Xouthos. Ion's speech (587-647) appears to be the opening speech in the debate: he sets out a clearly structured case giving separate objections to Xouthos' desire to take him back to Athens, and culminating in a political argument against kingship and in favour of a simple life. We therefore might expect Xouthos to defend his position. However, rather than rebutting Ion's points, or making a counter-case, he simply brushes Ion's speech aside and rejects the possibility of further debate: 'Enough of these arguments, learn to enjoy good fortune' (650). This derailing of the audience's expectations adds to the humour of the scene, and to the depiction of the relationship between Xouthos and Ion as cold and disengaged (see pp. 55-6 below). The effectiveness of the device, however, relies on the audience's knowledge of tragic conventions.

A final example occurs in the *deus ex machina* scene which ends the play. Divine intervention is a common feature in Euripidean tragedy, and usually occurs at the end of plays, where the gods provide some kind of resolution to the events on stage. Ion announces his intention to question Apollo, and so he is the god whom we expect to appear; instead, however, we are presented with Athene. That this is a reversal of our expectations is confirmed by the fact that Athene feels the need to justify her appearance (1556-9). The presence of Athene underscores Apollo's guilt, and suggests shame at his past actions. Despite Apollo's central importance, the play is framed with divine appearances by different deities, and his absence adds to our uncertainty about his true nature (see pp. 55-6).

Commentators on *Ion* are frequently struck by the sophistication and elegance of the play's structure.[25] The play is formed around different sets of repetitions, encouraging us to make connections between the two scenes or moments. Thus, we find two recognition scenes (Xouthos: Ion, 510-675; Creousa: Ion, 1395-1545), the first of which foreshadows the second, and informs our response to it. The play has two lyric monodies (by Ion, 82-183, and Creousa, 859-922) which fulfil a similar role in setting out each character's view of Apollo and of their own circumstances. Creousa is also given two antiphonal songs, one of which she sings with the Old Man/Chorus (763-99), and the other with Ion (1439-1509). Both these songs are sung in moments of extreme, and opposing, emotion, and they thus highlight the two sides of Creousa's nature, and the movement from hatred to joy she has undergone during the play. The emotional climax of the play, Creousa's murder attempt, is immediately followed by Ion's attempt to kill her, which links the two characters with a 'near miss' at the serious crime of kin-killing. Creousa's murder attempt is also paired with her original attempt to kill Ion by abandoning him as a baby: Creousa herself links the two events by seeing them as two separate betrayals by Apollo (912-15, 951-3). Finally, the play is framed by two divine appearances, emphasising the role of the gods in steering and controlling Ion's fate. The change from Hermes (Ion's childhood guardian) to Athene (patron god of his new city) emphasises Ion's own transition to maturity, as well as the movement from Delphi to Athens he is about to embark upon.

We can see therefore that the conventions of Greek tragedy, far from being restrictive, are used to create dramatic effects and to manipulate the audience's attitude to events. The audience's familiarity with these conventions, and the poets' skill at varying and manipulating them, makes them effective and flexible tools. Having placed *Ion* in its literary and historical context, what remains for us now is to examine the play's themes and preoccupations in closer detail.

3

Gods and Mortals

Questions about the nature of the gods and their role in human affairs are found throughout Greek literature. However, the subject matter of tragedy makes it a particularly appropriate genre to explore religious matters. Tragedy focuses on human suffering, and as such prompts its audience to question why we have to suffer, whether our fate is within our control, and how human suffering can be compatible with a system of divinely sanctioned justice. These issues are brought to the fore in *Ion*, a play in which divine intervention and will are prominent, and where the characters themselves question the morality of the gods' actions.

Modern readers have differed widely on their interpretation of the divine in the play. On the one hand, scholars have read the play as a criticism of established religion, and argue that through the play's presentation of Apollo as a somewhat dubious figure, Euripides encourages his audience to question traditional beliefs about the gods. Other scholars turn this reading on its head, and argue that Apollo is ultimately exonerated, and that the play's ending demonstrates the wisdom and beneficence of the gods.[1] This chapter will discuss how *Ion* presents the divine, and explore whether either of these readings is fully satisfactory. By examining what different characters say about religion and the gods, and the contexts in which they speak, we can investigate what conclusions the audience is led to.

Euripides and religion

Euripides is often felt to take a particular interest in portraying the gods, but it would be wrong to think that concerns about the gods were not central to Greek tragedy more generally: Aeschylus and Sophocles are also concerned with religious issues such as fate, human free will, and divine morality. What is true, however, is that these questions are posed more overtly and handled more self-consciously by Euripides. Gods appear on-stage more frequently in Euripidean tragedy than in plays by the other two tragedians (twelve of Euripides' seventeen surviving tragedies contain a divine appearance, compared to one of Aeschylus' six, and two of Sophocles' seven).[2] This has consequences in dramatic terms, since it means that the audience is given direct insight into the divine will. Whereas the human characters may perceive the gods' intentions as mysterious, the audience suffers from no such limitation, and can recognise when the mortal characters are mistaken in their interpretation of events.[3]

Another stylistic difference between the tragedians lies in the behaviour of the human characters. While lamenting the cruelty of fate may be a *topos* of Greek tragedy, Euripides' characters tend to be more vocal and articulate in their complaints about divine behaviour. In *Ion*, Apollo is attacked not only by Creousa, but also by Ion, who criticises the god in more general and philosophical terms for failing to set appropriate moral standards. We find similar arguments in other plays. At the end of *Bacchae,* Cadmus complains to Dionysus that his punishment has been excessive, arguing 'it is not right for gods to be like mortals in their anger' (1348), while the servant in *Hippolytus* claims that 'gods should be wiser than mortals' (120). Euripidean characters sometimes express doubt about traditional religious stories, or attempt to rationalise them. Thus, Helen expresses disbelief that she was really conceived by

Zeus taking the form of a swan (*Helen* 18-21), while Heracles refuses to accept that the gods have extra-marital affairs (*Heracles* 1341-6).

For this reason, Euripides' treatment of religion is often felt to be radical: his gods are seen as cruel and capricious, and as such disturbing to contemporary audiences and threatening to traditional religious belief. This portrayal has its origins in antiquity: in Aristophanes' *Women at the Thesmophoria*, a seller of religious garlands complains that Euripides' efforts have reduced belief in the gods and hence ruined her trade.[4] Many modern scholars continue to take this line, highlighting the overt criticism of divine behaviour that we find in Euripides' plays.[5] However, it is important not to overstate the gulf between Euripides and his literary predecessors.[6] Capricious gods date back to the *Iliad*, where the gods take sides in the war and help their human favourites, yet show little regard for human suffering. When Hera says to Zeus in *Iliad* 4 that if he allows her to destroy Troy, she will not begrudge him destroying any of her favourite cities (4.51-4), it is hard to see this arrangement as less cruel or capricious than any of Euripides' gods. Similarly, the idea of the immeasurable gulf between gods and men is prevalent in Homer: as the Homeric Apollo puts it, 'there can never be a likeness between the race of immortal gods, and of men who walk on the ground' (*Il.* 5.441-2). Because of this gap, the idea of applying mortal standards to the gods becomes problematic, for the gods are not accountable to mortals for their actions and face no consequences of the choices they make. Euripides' portrayal of vengeful gods is equally traditional, for the gods' punishments are frequently harsh, and often appear disproportionate on a human level. Poseidon's punishment of the Phaeacians for helping Odysseus in the *Odyssey* (13.149-58) seems just as disturbing as Dionysus' punishment of Cadmus and Agaue in *Bacchae*, as does the destruction of the whole city of Troy because of Paris' sin in abducting Helen. Viewed in this light, then, Euripides' gods are strikingly traditional: sometimes kind and sometimes vengeful, obsessed with their honour, and willing to crush mortals who disrespect them or their laws.[7]

What is true, however, is that the late fifth century saw the growth of a new intellectual movement, who were felt by traditionalists to be attacking (among other things) religious values.[8] These thinkers debated and questioned the morality of the traditional myths about the gods, as we see echoed in *Ion*. This school of thought is particularly evident in the writing of Plato. His dialogue *Euthyphro* begins with a man attempting to defend his assault on his father on the grounds that Zeus was said to have imprisoned his father, hence assuming that the same standards of morality should apply to men and gods (5e2-6a5). A fuller exposition of this theme is found in the *Republic*: Socrates points out the double standards between divine and mortal morality, suggests that gods would in fact never behave wrongly, and therefore concludes that poetry which depicts them doing such things should be banned (377e-391e). We have evidence elsewhere of friction over this type of religious question among the intellectual elite. Aristophanes' *Clouds* depicts a debate between Right and Wrong Argument, representing old-fashioned and new-fangled intellectual methods, where similar arguments are used (889-1104).[9] And the trial and execution of Socrates in 399 on a charge of impiety shows the depth of feeling that such debates could stir up.[10]

It is in this light that we should understand Euripides' presentation of the gods. Euripides is participating in a dialogue with those intellectuals who argue that traditional literary portrayals of the gods are misleading and inappropriate. As such, he presents these debates on stage, and characters in his plays (including Ion) frequently espouse the kind of view we find in contemporary thought. But Euripides' gods do not live up to these characters' aspirations: despite Ion's initial certainties about the gods, Apollo has in fact raped a woman, and Ion's pious assumptions about the nature of divinity are shown to be misguided. Similarly, in other Euripidean plays, characters who believe the gods should set a good example for mortals turn out to be wrong. The clearest example is in *Bacchae*, where Dionysus explicitly rejects Cadmus' suggestion that gods ought to be better than mortals. Instead, he accepts that his vengeance is excessive, but explains that he is following the natural order set up by Zeus (*Bacchae* 1346-9). Euripides' gods consistently behave in a manner reminiscent of, but more extreme than, flawed and fallible humans, obsessed with their honour and more concerned with their personal interests than any abstract notion of fairness. It does not follow from this, however, that Euripides portrays this conflict in beliefs in order to undermine the gods. Indeed, it would be just as natural to see Euripides' vengeful gods as a comment on the naivety of the rationalist school of thought, and an affirmation of the traditional literary portrayal of the gods.[11]

Religion in *Ion*

Having established these ideas, we can now move on to examine the presentation of the gods in *Ion*. The play is characteristically Euripidean in its engagement with the divine. The gods are prominent, and divine appearances frame the play. The nature of the gods is crucial to our understanding of the play's meaning, and debated explicitly by the characters.

It is Apollo who is central to the action of *Ion*, and whose character and behaviour is under scrutiny. The play is driven by two pieces of divine action: Apollo's rape of Creousa, and his subsequent decision to reunite mother and child. The prologue consists of a statement of Apollo's will, and the subsequent scenes show how his intentions are brought about. In addition, setting the play at Apollo's sanctuary in Delphi enhances the

relevance of the god: the shrine is Ion's home, and it is its oracular power that Creousa and Xouthos seek. Finally, the morality
of Apollo's actions is explicitly discussed by the characters:
Creousa and Ion both criticise the god, and Ion goes as far as to
generalise that gods and mortals ought not be judged by a
different set of standards (436-51) – a view which, as we have
seen, is commonly expressed by characters in Euripides.

Modern scholars have disagreed over the god's culpability.
Those who see the play as a critique of religion charge Apollo
with a variety of crimes: his rape of Creousa; his apparent
neglect of her and the baby; his incompetence in bringing his
plan to pass (whereby his decision to keep Creousa in ignorance
of Ion's identity nearly leads to the death of both characters);
his false oracle and continued deception of Xouthos. Others
attempt to defend the god from these charges: Apollo did not in
fact neglect Creousa or the baby, but worked to protect Ion and
to reunite him with his mother; the near failure of his plan is
due to human misunderstanding and bad luck, not to a fault in
the god.[12] They argue that divine rape, while abhorrent to a
modern reader, is standard mythological tradition, and is far
less problematic in a society which does not attribute the same
values to female consent and sexual rights as ours does. Finally,
the false oracle is a necessary evil to ensure Ion's position in
Athens, and to provide him with the benefits that a divine
father cannot.[13]

Many of these arguments are valid. However, any attempt to
whitewash Apollo runs into the problem that the play itself
presents a more nuanced view. For example, it is true that traditional myth does not present divine rape as morally
reprehensible, but Euripides problematises any attempt to
apply this moral view to the play by emphasising Creousa's pain
and grief. Similarly, the argument that Apollo has saved and
protected his son is anticipated by Ion, and forestalled by
Creousa's objection that in this case the god's secrecy would be

blameworthy: 'if he enjoys on his own joys which are to be shared, he acts unjustly' (358), to which Ion concedes 'the god is unjust then' (359). Simply arguing whether or not the charges made against Apollo are justifiable does not fully answer the question of how we are meant to respond to him. Since Apollo does not appear in the play; his actions and motivations are characterised entirely through other characters' attitudes towards them. Thus, in analysing statements made about Apollo in the play, we must take into account who makes these statements, and from what perspective. We should begin, therefore, by examining in detail how Apollo's actions are portrayed, and how the human characters respond to him.[14]

The first description of Apollo by a mortal is given by Ion, whose opening monody (82-183) expresses his love for the god. Ion has been brought up to serve Apollo, and his song describes his life in the temple and his delight at his tasks there. Ion describes his ritual duties in loving detail: purification at the sacred spring; cleansing the temple with a broom made of laurel (a plant sacred to Apollo); setting out garlands; preventing birds from polluting the temple. His descriptions of the sanctuary evoke a sense of calm and order, as well as suggesting the beauty and magnificence of the shrine. Ion also emphasises the joy he feels in performing these sacred duties: 'My labour is a glorious one; I am slave to no mortals but to the gods. I do not tire when I toil at my lucky work' (131-5).

The language Ion uses is evocative of real life piety. His description of cultic details (such as the Pythia sitting on her tripod and the burning of incense) reflect ritual at Delphi. His concern for purity also reflects Greek religious practice: pilgrims to Delphi would indeed be required to purify themselves at the sacred spring of Castalia before entering the sanctuary. Similarly, his warning to use appropriate language (98-101) is also founded in ritual practice: inauspicious language was believed to damage the ritual, and to bring bad luck. Ion's own language is full of words which would be considered religiously appropriate, signifying goodness, brightness, holiness, and beauty. The refrain 'Paian Apollo, Paian Apollo' (125-7 = 141-3) with which he ends his stanzas as he sweeps the temple is a tag-line taken from *paianes*: real cult songs for Apollo, which would, like Ion's song, have focussed on the beneficence and glory of the god.[15]

As well as its conventional piety, Ion's song also emphasises his personal devotion to the god. He calls Apollo his 'protector' and 'father', as well as his master, and twice describes how the temple provided him with shelter and nurture when he was a baby (109-11, 136-7). The joy at serving the god he expresses, therefore, is not merely pious convention, but personal emotion.

Ion's opening monody, then, sets up a model of Apollo as beneficent protector, and draws on the presentation of the god in real life cult to do so. However, his simple beliefs about the nature of Apollo are challenged when he hears Creousa's story. Ion's initial response is incredulity: Apollo's behaviour as she describes it is incompatible with his beliefs about the god. He refuses to accept that Apollo would have slept with a mortal woman, and suggests that Creousa's friend must be making up the story to cover up her shame at having been seduced by a mortal man (339-41).[16] He then warns Creousa against investigating the matter through the oracle, claiming that if this story is true, Apollo will be shamed if it is revealed, and it would be unwise to anger him (369-80). When Creousa and Xouthos leave, Ion attempts to put the subject out of his mind and return to his sacred tasks, but is unable to forget it (433-7). He then launches into a tirade against Apollo, complaining about his immoral behaviour and arguing that gods should abide by the standards they uphold for mortals: 'how can it be fair for you to enforce the laws for men, when you yourselves incur a charge of illegal behaviour?' (442-3).

Ion therefore explicitly rejects the idea of a gulf between gods and men; to him, the gods' superior power is all the more reason for them to act as good examples ('since you have power, pursue goodness', 439-40). His belief that the gods should abide by mortal standards is emphasised by his ironic suggestion that the gods ought to pay the appropriate fine for every rape they have committed, as a mortal rapist would be obliged to (444-7). His sharp criticism of Apollo here may appear to contrast with his earlier praise, but in fact both are founded on the same belief: namely, that the gods act perfectly justly. Apollo has fallen short of the standards Ion expects him to maintain, and as such, he chastises the god.

Ion's set of beliefs about Apollo, and his process of discovery about the true nature of the god, is paralleled by that of Creousa. When Creousa speaks with Ion on her initial entry, we become aware of her hostility towards Apollo. Ion is struck by the incongruity of her reaction to the temple ('everyone else rejoices when they see the halls of the god, but your eyes are overflowing with tears', 245-6). Criticisms of the god, more or less veiled, are scattered throughout Creousa's speech in this scene. She accuses Apollo of injustice, and of using his power to get away with his crimes (384-91). She bitterly acknowledges the superiority of the god: there is no higher power to which she can appeal (253-5), and as she is dependent on Apollo's good will to learn about the fate of her baby, she has no recourse if he does not wish to tell her (390-1).

Creousa's hostility to Apollo is brought out most strongly in her lyric monody (859-922), where she describes her rape and abandonment of her baby in detail. Like Ion in his monody, she draws on the traditional language of religion in her descriptions.[17] However, it is here used to achieve an ironic effect, setting the horror of Creousa's situation against the beauty and glory traditionally ascribed to the god. In religious poetry it is common to praise the god by naming his powers and the places associated with him.[18] Creousa addresses Apollo by listing two of his traditional roles: patron of music and god of prophecy (881-6, 907-10), and referring to his seats at Delos and Delphi, his two most important cult sites (907-10, 919-22). The language she uses is connected with each of the cults, referring to the delivery of oracles at Delphi, and the myth of Apollo's birth on Delos. However, this traditional language strikes an off-key note. Apollo's musical powers are contrasted with his behaviour in the play, as Creousa describes him playing the lyre as his son is killed:

> 'Now my son and yours is gone, snatched away by the birds for a feast. But you, hard-hearted that you are, jangle away on your cithara singing *paianes*.' (902-6)

Apollo's lyre-playing, rather than being an image of beauty and order, becomes a symbol for his abdication of his responsibilities to Creousa and his son.[19] Similarly, Apollo's role as prophet is contaminated by our knowledge that it is Apollo's use of his oracular power to give Xouthos a son which has prompted Creousa's fury. Finally, Creousa claims that Apollo's birthplace Delos, far from being a place of special honour for the god, hates and rejects him:

> 'Delos hates you, and so do the shoots of laurel by the delicate fronds of palm, where Leto bore you in the gardens of Zeus, in her sacred birth-pangs.' (919-22)

Creousa thus suggests that Apollo's unfair treatment of her and lack of care for her child is indicative of a lack of respect for parenthood. She therefore implies a corresponding lack of respect for his own birthplace, which accounts for Delos' hostility. In the light of this, her repeated invocation of the god as 'son of Leto' (885, 907) takes on new overtones. Whereas normally in religious poetry addressing the god by his parentage would be an honorific phrase, it now becomes a mechanism for highlighting his bad treatment of Creousa.

Like Ion, Creousa draws on real-life religious language and imagery to speak of the god. However, Creousa uses the norms of praise to condemn the god, not celebrate him. Whereas Ion's view of Apollo is that he is perfectly good, Creousa's is that he is wholly bad. Both characters are shown to be too simplistic in their understanding of the god, and both must learn by the end of the play to take a more nuanced view. Contrary to her own prediction earlier in the play, when she comments that even if Apollo were now to give her a child 'he would not be entirely dear to me' (425-7), Creousa abandons her anger when she is reunited with Ion. She acknowledges and then rejects her earlier hatred, instead expressing her gratitude to the god: 'I now praise Phoebus, though I didn't praise him before' (1609). She expresses her joy physically, caressing his temple and rejoicing in the sight of the shrine which earlier made her weep (1611-13).

Similarly, we see a change in Ion's view of Apollo, as he now has to accept that Apollo did rape a mortal girl and deliver a false oracle to Xouthos. His new mistrust is shown by his refusal to accept Creousa's explanation of why Apollo lied. Whereas he previously advised Creousa not to ask potentially embarrassing questions of the god in his temple, he now decides to confront Apollo directly (1546-8). Ion learns to accept that Apollo is less pure, and more pragmatic, than he had previously thought. He comes to see Apollo's mortal love-affair as a source of honour for himself, rather than a slur on the god's good name, and to see the false oracle as a clever solution to a problematic situation, rather than a religious impossibility. The picture of Apollo we are left with at the end of the play is not a whitewash: the god of the play is not the same perfect being of the god of Ion's initial prayer. However, neither is he a monster, and he is innocent of the charge laid against him with most venom: that he abandoned his son to die, and had no concern either for his future or for Creousa's. By following the figures of Ion and Creousa, and their opposite journeys in their understanding of Apollo, the audience too is encouraged to reach this more balanced conclusion about the god.[20]

Divine and mortal standards

On this reading one might be tempted to see the gods in *Ion* as fundamentally conventional, abiding by the literary tradition that portrays them as self-centred but nevertheless awe-inspiring. However, there is an important regard in which Apollo in the play differs from the conventions of literary gods. Whereas traditionally the gods are not held to the same standards as mortals, throughout the play there is an assumption by both mortal and divine characters that Apollo is to be judged by the same moral yardstick as a human. This theme is first and most prominently presented by Ion, who condemns Apollo for not abiding by conventional standards for correct behaviour (441-2). Taking this passage in isolation, we might choose to attribute it to Ion's naivety about the divine. However, on closer analysis, this idea recurs throughout the play.

A clear example of this is the portrayal of Creousa's rape and pregnancy.[21] According to mythological convention, bearing a god's child is a source of honour for the woman selected, and for her family. For example, Pindar in his ninth Pythian Ode selects the myth of Apollo's seduction of the maiden Cyrene in order to praise the city named after her. Cyrene (and other girls in her situation) is not tainted by the sexual contact, nor does it present any problems for her social status.[22] Rather, the divine rape, and subsequent birth, is viewed as a happy ending. This aspect of traditional myth is stressed by scholars who want to see the play as affirming Apollo's ultimate goodness; they argue that modern objections to the rape are a result of our anachronistic interpretation both of women's rights and of the nature of divinity. However, this convention is deliberately overturned in the play. Far from rejoicing in the divine favour shown her, Creousa sees the rape as a source of shame. She responds exactly as though she had been made pregnant by a mortal man, seeing it as necessary to conceal the pregnancy and get rid of the baby: at 898 she speaks of her fear at giving birth to a child.[23] The incongruity of this situation is highlighted by Ion's response to the story: when Creousa tells him that her 'friend' suffered terribly as a result of her unexpected pregnancy (342), he replies in surprise 'What did she do to suffer, if she had intercourse with a god?' (343). We see a similar tendency in Ion's conviction that Creousa (or the woman in her story) must in fact have been raped by a mortal and attributed the blame to Apollo in order to hide her shame (341, 1522-7).

The presentation of Apollo as a mortal seducer is further highlighted by the secrecy in which the play ends. It is reasonable to explain Apollo's false oracle to Xouthos as a case of the ends justifying the means. However, this raises the question why Xouthos should have to be kept in the dark. Creousa explains to Ion that Xouthos would not accept the boy as his heir if he knew he was not his son (1539-45): again, this is the logic of the real world, not of religious myth, where the children of divine rapes are frequently given a mortal surrogate father to oversee their upbringing. Sharing a marriage bed with a god and being selected to raise a semi-divine child is usually a mark of honour, which Xouthos ought to rejoice in. Euripides thus deliberately takes a traditional religious story and turns its values on their head. The circumstances of Ion's birth are presented as part of a contemporary 'rationalising' world, where a divine rape appears to be the stuff of fairy-tale, and nothing more than a convenient lie for a fallen woman to tell.

The play's ending, moreover, makes it clear that it is not only the mortal characters who assume an equivalence between divine and mortal values. Athene explains that Apollo's absence results from anxiety as to how the humans might respond to him: 'he did not think it right to appear before the two of you, in case blame for the past should be openly expressed, and he sent me to tell you this message' (1557-8). Apollo's motivation implies a sense of shame at being confronted with his past actions; it also suggests a concern for what mortals think of him. This is highly uncharacteristic of the gods of traditional literature: we might compare the Homeric presentation of Apollo, who tells Poseidon, 'you would not say I was of sound mind if I fought you for the sake of wretched mortals', contrasting the immortality of the gods with the transient nature of human life (*Iliad* 21.462-6). A close parallel to Apollo's situation in *Ion* is Dionysus in Euripides' *Bacchae*, who is criticised by the mortal characters for his excessive vengeance, but is unconcerned by their complaints, and simply asserts his divine authority (1346-9). There are of course other reasons for Athene's appearance: her presence alludes to his new status as an Athenian rather than Delphian citizen. However, having Athene herself explain her presence as covering for Apollo's embarrassment draws attention to his unwillingness to confront the mortals. In the play, then, the claim that gods should respect the ethical standards they lay down for men is taken seriously by the divine as well as the mortal characters.

Ion thus picks up and explores the contention surrounding divine and mortal values. The play explores what might happen if the divine behaviour of traditional myth really were judged by human standards. This premise is certainly an unconventional one, and as such the audience would no doubt have found it striking. However, to interpret this as a serious attack on the values of traditional myth is to overlook the play's tone: the application of realistic values to heroic myth in the play is usually humorous. In the world of myth, women are frequently raped by gods, but an Athenian audience-member would hardly accept it as an excuse for a questionable pregnancy from his own wife. Ion thus treats Creousa with a suspicion which would be normal in the real world, but is inappropriate in the mythological one, and by doing so creates a humorous tension between the two systems. Similarly, the idea of a powerful god having to sneak around behind the back of a cuckolded husband is intrinsically funny. Nevertheless, the play handles serious ideas, and the issues around traditional beliefs are those which were being debated among intellectuals. But while the play may question traditional beliefs, it does not attack or challenge them. Apollo's behaviour may be open to criticism, but the play's upbeat ending encourages us to accept it, as Creousa does. The paradox of a powerful god being treated like a human highlights the absurdity of the play's premise. *Ion* suggests that the gods are neither perfectly good nor monstrously evil, but reaffirms the gulf between them and mortal men.

4

Mothers and Children

To the Greeks, producing children who could ensure the continuity of the family line was of immense importance. In Herodotus' *Histories*, when the sage Solon is asked to identify the most fortunate man on earth, he picks an ordinary citizen, and gives as one of the main reasons for calling him happy that he is the father of fine sons, who went on to have children of their own.[1] The theme of parenthood, and the nature of the bond between parent and child, is the most prevalent theme of *Ion*. All the characters recognise the importance of children, and parenthood lies at the heart of the play's action. The most repeated and vitriolic of the criticisms aimed at Apollo throughout the play is the accusation that he ignored his obligations as a father and left his son to die.[2] In fact, it is the god's concern to ensure his son's welfare that drives the plot and leads to Ion's adoption into Xouthos' household. Conversely, Creousa and Xouthos' frustration at their childlessness is the reason for their journey to Delphi. And this frustration, combined with outrage at Apollo's apparent bad treatment of his own child, is sufficient to propel Creousa towards murder.

This chapter will explore the way that the parent-child relationship is presented in *Ion*, and the assumptions that the characters make about parenthood. The play raises questions about what constitutes a parent: is it simply the biological parent of the child, the provider of sustenance, or a combination? It also explores the separate rights and responsibilities within the family that mother and father hold, and to which parent the child owes more loyalty. Feminist readers of *Ion* have seen the conflict between mother's and father's rights as central to the way that gender is presented in the play, and to the portrayal of Creousa. Creousa's crisis is prompted by motivations which are traditionally female ones: a desire to protect her household and her status within the home. The degree to which the play condones her actions and the way that her desire for vengeance is presented are therefore significant in determining the attitude to women which it presents.

What makes a parent?

Various scholars have noted that *Ion* encourages its audience to question the nature of parenthood by exploring on what basis the title of 'parent' can be conferred.[3] During the play, four characters are named as Ion's mother or father: Creousa, Apollo, the Pythia, and Xouthos. Between them, these four have performed the components that make up parenthood. Creousa is the biological parent, the Pythia oversaw the child's upbringing, and Xouthos provides the grown child with public recognition, acting as a mechanism to integrate him into the wider community. Apollo's status is less clearly defined, for he acts both as Ion's biological father and (indirectly) as his nurturer, and is given the title of father in both roles.

What scholars who see the play as problematising parenthood overlook, however, is that *Ion* itself resolves these conflicting claims by prioritising the role of the blood-parent. Surrogate parents, while important, are consistently represented as failing to provide something for the child. Conversely, although Creousa the blood-parent has played no role in the child's upbringing, the relationship between her and Ion is not depicted as lacking in any way. [4]

This can be seen more clearly by a closer analysis of the play

itself, and of the key moments when these issues are explored
and debated. Ideas about parenthood are first presented in
Ion's monody, when the boy describes his own upbringing and
relationship to Apollo and the shrine. Ion repeatedly suggests
that Apollo and his temple have fulfilled the role of parents for
him, and on this basis calls the god his father:

> 'Phoebus is my father who begot me. For I praise the one who
> feeds me, and the name of father, my benefactor, I give to
> Phoebus who rules this shrine.' (136-40)

The word which Ion uses here (*genetôr*) means 'begetter'; Ion is
suggesting that Apollo's provision for him makes him equivalent to a blood parent, and hence that the nature of parenthood
derives from the social and economic role that a parent fulfils
for their child. This is consistent with the line Ion takes earlier
in the song, where he explains that in the absence of parents,
his duties are to the temple: 'for since I was born motherless
and fatherless, I serve the temple of Phoebus that reared me'
(109-11).

However, the case Ion makes is undermined by his own
awareness that Apollo's relationship to him does not constitute
true parenthood. It is significant that he simultaneously
describes himself as 'fatherless', and calls Apollo his father. The
god may have provided for him generously, but we are nevertheless led to feel that prioritising this aspect of the parental
relationship is unsatisfactory. Ion expresses much the same
attitude at the end of the play when he greets the Pythia who
raised him: 'Greetings, dear mother – though it was not you
who gave me birth' (1324). Ion's language suggests a paradox in
calling the priestess his mother, and her reply acknowledges
that the title is incorrect in an important sense: 'Well, anyway,
that's what I'm called, and the expression doesn't offend me'
(1325). The relationship between Ion and the Pythia is depicted

as that of mother and child: she repeatedly calls the boy 'son', and gently rebukes him for his anger, while Ion accepts her guidance, commenting 'what you say will be spoken from a kind heart' (1336). However, despite the mutual fondness both characters express, both nevertheless imply a deficiency in their relationship.

The preference for blood relationship over social one is further explored in Ion's scene with Creousa. Euripides depicts a strong natural bond between the two characters which overcomes the lack of any existing relationship, and which we must infer springs from their kinship.[5] Ion is immediately drawn to Creousa on her entrance, admiring her appearance and moved by her obvious sadness. His cry of amazement upon noticing her tears ('oh, you amaze me', 241) highlights the impact that Creousa has on him: the Greek word he uses of his reaction (*exeplêxas*) is normally used of strong emotions. Both Ion and Creousa express curiosity about each other, seeking to find out the other's history. Their bond is further expressed by the sympathy each feels for the other's sorrows. Ion is immediately able to recognise the magnitude of Creousa's suffering over her childlessness, while Creousa expresses her pity for Ion, abandoned and ignorant of his history (312, 320). In addition, Creousa and Ion construct their relationship around the roles of mother and son. In Creousa's initial question to Ion, her compliment to him is couched in terms of his relationship to his mother ('how happy your mother must be', 308). Her interest in his story focuses on this relationship: she expresses pity for his mother's plight (324), and feels particular sympathy when Ion tells her he was never fed at a woman's breast. Like Ion, Creousa also recognises a bond between the two of them, and suggests that their sufferings are of a similar nature (319). Ion's emotional involvement in Creousa's story is further stressed by his reaction after she and Xouthos leave the stage. Ion attempts to return to his duties in the temple, but is unable to stop

thinking about Creousa's troubles, and tries to remind himself
where his loyalties ought to lie:

'But what concern of mine is the daughter of Erechtheus? She's
got nothing to do with me. No, I will go and pour water into the
vessels with my golden jugs' (433-6)

The irony of these lines is enhanced by the fact that the Greek
word *prosêkein* ('to do with') can also mean 'be related to'. The
implication is that Ion unknowingly responds to his blood-
relationship with his mother, and that this relationship is
important, even though until now mother and son have had
nothing to do with one another.

A direct comparison between different types of parental relationship is further developed by the contrast between Ion's
interaction with Creousa and that with Xouthos. Whereas
Creousa and Ion's first encounter demonstrated natural close-
ness and warmth, Ion's interaction with Xouthos is marked by
coldness and mutual misunderstanding.[6] Rather than being
moving, the recognition scene is humorous, and we are encouraged to laugh at Xouthos rather than to share his joy at
discovering a son. The humour is accentuated by the difference
in emotional tone between Ion and Xouthos. Xouthos' enthusiastic attempts to embrace his new son are interpreted by Ion as
inappropriate personal contact from a stranger; Ion reacts to
this excessive friendliness with equally excessive hostility,
threatening to attack Xouthos if he does not leave him alone
('let go, before you get an arrow through your ribs', 524).[7] While
Xouthos assumes Ion will quickly believe he is his father, Ion
in fact takes his claim to be a joke. He is only convinced with
difficulty, after exploring all possible alternatives, such as
suggesting that Xouthos has misunderstood the oracle (533).
Ion's eventual acceptance that Xouthos must be his father is
presented as a series of logically forced steps, rather than a

joyous discovery, and comes about as a response to Xouthos' explicit request that Ion acknowledge him (556-61). He first concedes that he must believe Apollo, then somewhat grudgingly admits that there is some benefit in a father descended from Zeus. Having agreed that Xouthos must be his father, he then concedes that he ought to touch him. He finally acknowledges Xouthos, but his greeting is formal and without emotion, consisting of only half a line ('Greetings, father', 561).

Ion's scene with Xouthos foreshadows his later recognition scene with Creousa, and there are many linguistic and dramatic similarities between the two. These similarities, however, are used to emphasise the difference in tone that the two scenes achieve. For example, both Xouthos and Creousa respond to discovering Ion with a desire for physical contact. In both cases, the boy initially reacts with horror, and accuses them of behaving madly. However, when convinced that Creousa is his mother, far from acquiescing coldly, Ion reacts to her embrace with joy and returns her kisses (1437-8, 1443-4). In both scenes, Ion thinks about the other parent, and asks about the story of his birth. With Creousa, though, he does not raise the subject of his father until they have expressed their joy at finding each other. When he does so, he introduces the topic diplomatically, suggesting that it is unkind to exclude his father (who he still assumes is Xouthos) from their mutual joy: 'Mother, my father ought to be here and share in the pleasure that I have given to the two of you' (1468-9).

Ultimately, while Creousa is given total claim to be Ion's mother, his paternity is shared between Apollo and Xouthos, the latter continuing to provide the social and public aspects of fatherhood, while the former's biological claim is kept secret. It might be tempting to read this as an acknowledgment of the importance of both aspects of parenthood, and an equivocation over which, if either, is more important. However, the deception which surrounds the division of Ion's paternity belies this reading. As we have already seen, this deception is unconventional. Gods are not able to provide an upbringing for a mortal child and so frequently choose mortal surrogates to perform the social aspects of parenthood for their offspring: as far as the human father is concerned, his lack of biological paternity is nothing to be ashamed of. For example, Zeus and Amphitryon share the paternity of Heracles, and in Euripides' *Heracles*, Amphitryon attacks Zeus not on the grounds that the affair was immoral *per se*, but because the god fails to respect his obligations as Heracles' father to protect his son (339-47). In *Ion*, however, we are told that Xouthos will not be prepared to fulfil his role as social parent unless he believes that the biological paternity is also his. This is not simply a matter of Ion's legal status as heir, for there is nothing to prevent Xouthos willingly adopting Ion, as Creousa suggests in the analogy she uses to explain Apollo's plan to Ion: 'thus indeed a man might give his own son to his friend, to be an heir to his house' (1535-6). This analogy in fact highlights the dissimilarity with Ion's situation. Apollo is not entering into a contract of friendship and Xouthos would not accept Ion as his heir, as Creousa herself acknowledges:

> 'Apollo is doing you a favour by establishing you in a noble house. For if you were said to be the god's son, you would get neither the full inheritance of the house nor the name of a father.' (1540-3)

Xouthos and Apollo both attribute a status to biological parentage, therefore, which social parentage does not have: the social advantage, we infer, is dependent on the biological connection. It is also important that Ion turns out to be biologically an Athenian: a coincidence which makes his social incorporation as the heir of the ruling family acceptable. The play does not ignore the importance of the public aspect of parenting: Ion, Creousa, Xouthos and Apollo all show an acute awareness of the issues faced by a child who lacks this grounding. But in the end, the social integration parents provide is presented as something convenient and able to be manipulated: it is Ion's search for his biological parents that lies at the play's emotional heart.

Mothers and fathers

Another polarity which dominates issues about parenthood in the play is that of mother/father. Here too, scholars are divided on the relative importance the play attributes to each parent. Rabinowitz, for example, argues that *Ion* resolves the question in favour of the father, and that Ion's development shows a shift in attachment from the mother to the father. However, this is to overlook the strong bond between Ion and Creousa, and the contrast that Euripides draws between this and the boy's relationship with Xouthos. This difference cannot only be explained in terms of the natural power of a blood relationship: Ion is also more concerned to discover his mother than his father, demonstrated most strikingly by his urgent questioning of Xouthos about his mother's identity.

When Ion realises that Xouthos must know who his mother is, we see a shift in the tone of the dialogue: Ion now pursues this line of questioning vigorously, leaving any further acknowledgement of Xouthos' role until he realises he will learn no more about his mother.[8] Once he has been convinced that Xouthos' claim is right, he returns again to think about his mother, and his affectionate language forms a striking contrast with his cold acknowledgment of Xouthos: 'Dear mother, when shall I see your form? Now I long to know who you are more than before' (563-4). He goes as far as to suggest that his life will be 'unliveable' if he does not discover his mother's identity (670). Ion perceives the discovery of a father in terms of public and social status: he is glad that Xouthos can trace his ancestry back to Zeus, but fears for his status as an illegitimate son. Conversely, whilst he is not entirely oblivious to the social implications of his mother's identity (for example, he is glad to learn he is free-born (556) and hopes his mother will turn out to be an Athenian (670-5)), his desire to discover his mother is presented as arising from emotional motives. His response to learning his true birth is similar in tone: 'Mother, finding you is a dear discovery, and there's no fault to be found with my genealogy' (1518-19).

This prioritisation of the mother is further enhanced by Euripides' treatment of the myth, and the way he chooses to develop the plot. Creousa dominates the stage both in terms of number of lines and the emotional intensity of her scenes; Xouthos, on the other hand, is a relatively minor character. While Creousa's reunion with her son is the culmination of the action, Xouthos' merely forms its comic foil. Creousa's ignorance about her baby's fate is the most poignant aspect of the play, whereas Xouthos' deception at the end is glossed over. The play celebrates the strength of the mother-child bond, while mocking the father's pretensions to know his own child. Indeed, the normal rules of inheritance are reversed, for while Ion is publicly acknowledged as Xouthos' son, it is in fact his maternal line which validates his claim to the Athenian throne.

Choosing the female side is to some extent surprising. Aeschylus' *Eumenides* features a debate about the rights of father and mother, coming firmly down on the father's side: a decision almost certainly less startling to the Greeks than to a modern audience. Children were conceptualised as the property of the father, and in literature, vengeful women such as Medea and Hecuba identify harming the children as the most effective punishment for wicked men. In law, the decision on whether to raise a newborn child was that of the male head of the household.[9] The play itself acknowledges the greater importance traditionally placed on the father-child relationship. Xouthos is surprised by his son's insistence on knowing who his mother is: it is not something that has occurred to him as being important enough to ask the oracle about (541). Apollo too is unprepared for Ion's insistence on discovering his mother, and did not volunteer any information to Xouthos on the subject. Apollo's plan centres on the social primacy of the father-child bond: he presumed that Xouthos and Ion will be content to ask no further questions, and that Creousa will accept her husband's son into her household. The plan is based on the fear that Xouthos will reject Ion if he knows him not to be his son, but assumes that Creousa will have no such problems.[10]

However, we must not lose sight of the importance of a Greek woman's position in the *oikos* (home, or family unit), and her role as wife and mother within it. Literary characters such as Orestes and Oedipus show us the power attributed to the mother-child relationship, and the particular horror of its perversion.[11] In more concrete terms, the mother's role in assuring the status of the child, and thus her own status in the household, was enshrined in law. The Citizenship Decree of 451 BC made it compulsory to have two freeborn Athenian parents in order to qualify for citizenship. The wife's role within the family was thus affirmed, and in the years following this decree, we find an increase in the depictions of women in art, suggesting awareness of the importance of their role.[12] Similarly, under Athenian law, marriage was allowed between half-siblings who shared a father but not between those who shared a mother, suggesting a particular importance to the mother-child relationship.[13] For an Athenian audience of Euripides' day, then, knowing the identity of your mother was of paramount importance.

We should therefore avoid reading the affirmation of motherhood in *Ion* as a proto-feminist stance which subverts male values. To do so would be to ignore the value that Greek culture placed on the mother-child bond. Problems and jokes around establishing paternity are well ingrained in Greek culture (as many others), and can be traced back to the *Odyssey*, where Telemachus says to Athene that 'my mother says I am [Odysseus]' son, but I don't know – no one can be sure of his own parentage' (*Od.* 1.215-6). In addition, Xouthos is portrayed as a cuckold, and as such is a traditional figure of fun. As an outsider whose claim to his throne is dependent on his wife, he is doubly ridiculous. His emasculation is completed by his attempt to smuggle in an illegitimate son without his wife's knowledge: an offence usually associated with females.[14] Taking the deception of Xouthos as a serious attack on masculinity would be like interpreting Aristophanes' *Assembly-Women* as a serious suggestion that women should take over political power. Conversely, Creousa's concern with children and with her own fertility is entirely feminine. The seriousness of her feelings for her child, and of his desire to find a mother, are equally traditional. The special emotional bond between mothers and children dates back to the *Iliad*, where Andromache is depicted as deeply concerned for the welfare of her child. Nor does this bond cease when the child becomes an adult man, for we also see Hecuba try to persuade Hector to remain in Troy, and Thetis continually providing comfort and support to Achilles.[15] It is true that the play picks up on and explores genuine issues of concern to the audience surrounding gender and family relationships. But it does so in a way that affirms the importance of the family unit, and whose elements of deceit and subversion are light-hearted.

Women, wives, and mothers

Greek tragedy frequently focuses on strong female characters, and *Ion* is no exception. Despite the play's title, Creousa is arguably the main character in dramatic and emotional terms, and it is her shifts in mood which dictate the tone of the play. Euripides' interest in powerful women was noted in antiquity, and in *Women at the Thesmophoria*, Aristophanes makes the women cast Euripides as a misogynist, claiming that Euripides has damaged their reputation and revealed their secrets.[16] Most modern scholars would take a more nuanced view, pointing out how many of Euripides' plays encourage us to sympathise with women who might easily be portrayed as unsympathetic monsters (for example Medea or Phaedra).[17] Creousa shares many of the characteristics of these other tragic females, notably her extreme emotions and her desire for vengeance. In analysing how the play presents Creousa, and women more generally, we must look not only at Creousa herself, but at the wider patterns surrounding the way women are portrayed in tragedy.

In Greek culture, producing children was considered the goal of a woman's life.[18] The words of the betrothal ceremony tell us that a woman was given to her new husband 'for the ploughing [i.e. production] of legitimate children', and female development was conceptualised as culminating in the birth of a child, which marked the woman's irreversible passage to maturity and into her marital household.[19] The importance Creousa attaches to her fertility is therefore unsurprising. It is significant that what drives her into a murderous state of mind is not only Xouthos' adoption of Ion, but the Chorus' embellishment of the oracle to mean that she will never produce any children (761-2). Infertility would be legitimate grounds for divorce, an idea picked up in the play when the old man suggests that rather than smuggling in Ion, Xouthos should have taken another wife in view of Creousa's sterility (839-42). While Xouthos himself never suggests that he will divorce Creousa or harm her in any other way, Creousa's fears are understandable: it would be wrong to explain them away as irrational or melodramatic.

It is important that we do not entirely lose sympathy for Creousa, as the end of the play would be ineffective if we were not able to share in her joy at her transformed situation. The murder-attempt, therefore, is described with various mitigating circumstances. Firstly, it is significant that Creousa acts in ignorance of her true relationship to Ion: unlike Medea or Clytemnestra, her actions are performed in the belief that she is protecting her *oikos*, not destroying it. Our desire that her plan should fail, therefore, comes as much from sympathy for Creousa as for Ion: his murder would result in further misery for Creousa, not in victory. The murder of a family-member is always portrayed as a perversion of the natural order; hatred towards a stepson, on the other hand, is portrayed as natural, even if a murder attempt is inherently repulsive. The play indicates that Creousa's fear is in fact misplaced: Ion has no desire to evict Creousa, and is acutely aware of the difficult situation his presence will put her in (607-20). Nevertheless, hostility between stepmother and stepchild is a commonplace of Greek culture (and many others). In Euripides' *Alcestis*, the eponymous heroine makes her husband promise not to remarry after her death, on the grounds that a new wife will be harmful to her children (304-16); similarly, one of the arguments the Nurse in *Hippolytus* uses to encourage her mistress to live is that she needs to protect her legitimate children's interests against her stepson (305-10). In *Ion,* Creousa's hostility towards Ion is taken as read. The Pythia justifies Creousa's hatred, implying that Ion is wrong to object to it: 'Wives are always hostile to stepsons' (1329). Ion himself has already anticipated Creousa's distress at his incorporation into her household, and argues that it will be justifiable: 'How will she not hate me – and rightly so?' (611).

Creousa's murderous mindset is presented as something incited by others, rather than simply being a result of her character. Creousa's own response to learning about Xouthos' adoption of Ion is pain and distress: it is the old slave who encourages her to take revenge (843-6, 970-9). Even so, Creousa rejects the old man's suggestion that she kill Xouthos as well as Ion, recalling that Xouthos has been a good husband in the past, and speaking of the respect she feels for their marriage (977). The pragmatic nature of Creousa's crime is thus highlighted, as well as her essential goodness: while Ion poses a genuine threat to Creousa's position, killing Xouthos would be purely an act of vengeance, and an excessive one at that. It is also significant that Creousa herself is not directly involved in the murder attempt: the old man insists that she delegate the task to him. Thus she is a step removed from the direct act of killing, and her connection with the crime becomes more tenuous.

Creousa's monody (859-922) is also important in maintaining the sympathetic aspects of her character. We are shown the level of pain Creousa has suffered both from the original rape and now from what she understandably sees as a betrayal by Apollo.[20] The monody reaffirms that we are meant to regard the rape (and putative abandonment of the baby) as moral crimes, not simply as mythological back-story. The monody emphasises Creousa's fear and distress when she was raped, and also her sorrow and regret at the baby's death. We are reminded that, from Creousa's point of view, Apollo has neglected his responsibilities as a father and as a lover, and thus are brought to understand why Apollo's attempt to integrate an illegitimate child into her house is a step too far.

Nevertheless, the ending of the play relies on intense hostility between Creousa and Ion. For this reason, it is important that the audience takes Creousa's murderous intentions seriously: the threat she poses must be a real one, and she must be personally committed to the success of her plan, whether or not she is distanced from carrying it out. In portraying Creousa, Euripides uses language reminiscent of other vengeful females of tragedy, whose revenge is usually portrayed as excessive and terrifying.[21] However conventional Creousa's emotions, her desire to take action is less acceptable. A Greek woman was not expected to take matters into her own hands or to rebel against the wishes of her male kinsmen.[22] 'Good' women in tragedy may have strong opinions, and may attempt to persuade the male characters of them, but they do not act independently, and women's attempts to take action usually end in disaster.[23]

Like other tragic females, Creousa is unable to take vengeance directly, or to use masculine or 'heroic' means such as the sword. Creousa herself rejects the slave's suggestion that she arrange for overt violence, by equipping her slaves with swords (983). Instead, like Medea or Deaneira, she turns to a potion, and like them, one of supernatural origin. This association with witchcraft is further highlighted by the Chorus' ode which follows the scene, where they call upon Hecate, goddess of magic, to assist Creousa in her plot (1048-60). In aligning herself with these forces, Creousa becomes more monstrous; as she obtains supernatural power, the sympathy she has obtained as a defenceless victim is also undermined.

The 'feminine' nature of Creousa's crime is also stressed. The old man suggests that vengeance and murder within the family is a tendency typical of women:

'Now you must do something truly female – kill your husband and the boy, either with a sword or by deceit or poison.' (843-5)

This is enhanced by Creousa's complicity with the Chorus. At the start of the scene where she turns from victim to would-be murderess, she addresses them as 'women, faithful slaves of my loom and shuttle' (747-8). The implication is a natural bond between women which overrides the gulf between freeborn and slave. By referring to the loom, Creousa evokes traditional female activities that unite them, as she begs the Chorus to tell her what Xouthos has learned from the oracle. The Chorus respond by disobeying Xouthos' orders and revealing his secret. Their loyalty to their mistress is stressed throughout, and they see the adoption as a betrayal of Creousa, as well as of Athens. The choral ode after the plotting scene further emphasises the alliance of women against men. The Chorus criticise the male control of poetry which has led to women's reputation for sexual unfaithfulness. Arguing that men in fact behave worse than women, they call on the Muse of poetry to bring to light men's infidelity (1090-8). That this passage consists of a piece of sung poetry indicates that the Chorus' wish is coming true: their song becomes the female poetic voice that they wish for. This female complicity adds to a sense of threat: the women incite each other to overturn the system, and to take vengeance for past wrongs. It therefore enhances the sinister overtones of Creousa's vengeance, implying a fundamental hostility between men and women, and a threat posed by women to male norms and structures.[24]

If Creousa's vengeance is characteristically female, we must consider what impact this has on the portrayal of gender relationships within the play. Euripides frequently depicts powerful female figures, and commentators are divided over how we should interpret these characters. The plays showcase their admirable qualities as well as their flaws, and as with Creousa, we are led to understand what drives these women to commit crimes, and to sympathise with their position. Feminist commentators, however, stress the way that the plays ultimately uphold the dominant male ideology.[25] Females like Creousa, who transgress, are motivated by emotion, suggesting the importance of rationality and self-control, traditionally considered male virtues. Froma Zeitlin goes further, suggesting the function of females in tragedy is to offer moral lessons to and about men: women, she argues, are catalysts to the action of tragedy, rather than ends in themselves; and the plays' ultimate focus is an exploration of the male self.[26] This seems to go rather too far; even if one argues that the purpose of the play is to tell the story of Ion's rise to greatness, the audience's experience focuses largely on Creousa's suffering. The outcome of the play is just as much her gain of a child as Ion's discovery of an identity.

What is true, however, is that tragic females are frequently presented as behaving as they do as a result of the actions of men. In tragedy, women tend to be problematic as a result of their failure to conform to normal gender roles. Thus, we are shown examples of women who kill their husbands rather than obeying them (Clytemnestra), or women who murder rather than nurturing children (Medea). Frequently, though, when women break these norms, it is to a great extent caused by the disruption to their legitimate roles brought about by males. Thus, Medea's murderous rage is a result of Jason's abandonment of his marriage; Clytemnestra's hatred of her husband is (at least partly) caused by his murder of their daughter, and thus the disruption of her rights as a mother. Similarly, when women are presented as sympathetic victims, our pity is elicited by the denial of their expectations as women: for example, Iphigeneia is denied a marriage; Andromache is unable to protect and raise her child.[27] *Ion* fits this pattern well, for Creousa's murderous side is brought out by her husband trying to usurp her status as legitimate wife by bringing in his own illegitimate son. Creousa is more unambiguously sympathetic than many of these tragic females, partly because she acts in ignorance, but largely because her vengeance is never fulfilled. However, the similarities between Creousa and the more disturbing women of Greek tragedy are important, for the factors that motivate them and pressures acting upon them are shown to be similar. Because Creousa's plot is foiled, and the play ends in joy rather than destruction, we are encouraged to view her sympathetically, and to see how a good wife and virtuous woman could be driven to murder. The moral outcome is reassuring, for the play suggests that disruption within the *oikos* is caused by a failure to respect the proper roles of all participants.

Ion begins with a dysfunctional family: a childless couple; a parentless boy; a woman unable to fulfil the purpose of her existence, and a man whose public and political authority is dependent on his wife. By the end of the play, these defects have been corrected. Mother and son are reunited, and the split in Ion's paternity is smoothed over by the deception of Xouthos. Creousa has discharged her obligation to provide a son, and the new heir to the Athenian throne is invested with authority in his own right. The chaotic events of the play explores what can happen when the ordinary codes and values that govern family relationships break down, and its ending demonstrates the importance of restoring the correct balance. Creousa demonstrates how even a good woman can become bad if her legitimate rights are ignored, but her reconciliation with Ion at the end shows the possibility of harmony within the family, and the importance of this balance in creating successful human relationships.

Identity and Empire

Ion hinges on a boy's quest to discover his own identity, and follows his journey from nameless waif to prince and founding father. As we saw in the previous chapter, the acquisition of an identity is explored in part through ideas about parenthood: discovering his true parents is presented as the key to Ion's search for who he is. The play thus upholds the importance of origins in establishing an identity. Ion seeks an explanation of how he came to be, and needs to know the narrative of his own conception. Moreover, Ion's personal identity is inextricably linked to his acquisition of an Athenian identity. Through the responses of the play's characters to this discovery, Euripides explores what it means to be Athenian. The plot of *Ion* is thus a foundation myth, for it forms part of the history of the original royal house, and explains Athens' links to the Ionian Greeks. The play also stresses the symbolism of Ion's story by using imagery which assimilates it to the history of Athens.

Individual identity: the journey to adulthood

Ion's story is presented not just as a search for truth, but as a process of claiming a new identity as an adult. His departure from the shrine is presented as a form of rebirth; the feast which symbolises his acceptance by Xouthos is portrayed as though it were a birth feast, and the words used of the offerings Xouthos makes (*genethlia,* 653, *optêria,* 1127) normally signify the rituals conducted at the birth of a child.[1] The anthropologist van Gennep identified a common pattern for rites of passage and transition across many cultures, whereby such rituals frequently involve a symbolic death followed by a reincorporation into a new status.[2] The transition to maturity often contains some form of symbolic danger or ordeal, actualised in *Ion* by Creousa's attempt on the boy's life. The play thus traces Ion's journey from boyhood to manhood, and shows him coming to terms with his new status and leaving the life he knows.

Ion's life at the shrine is presented as an idyllic childhood world of purity and innocence, where his only responsibilities are to the god he regards as a father. In going to Athens, he must enter the adult world and take his place in society. His initial response to Xouthos suggests his reluctance to make this transition. He stresses his happiness at Delphi and the pleasures of life there: he has leisure and is surrounded by piety and joy (633-44). He rejects the life of politics and kingship and begs Xouthos to allow him to stay at the shrine (646-7). By the end of the play, however, he accepts that he must depart for Athens and welcomes his status as future ruler:

> *Athene*: 'Take your seat on the throne of Athens.'
> *Ion*: 'It is a worthy possession, I think.' (1618)

Political participation was considered an essential part of adulthood and social responsibility in fifth-century Athens: the concept of 'living a quiet life' was viewed as suspect, and as tantamount to rejecting the values of the *polis*.[3] While the play presents a fictional world of monarchs rather than a fifth-century democracy, Ion's description of political affairs, with its focus on democratic debate and political rivalries, seems to draw just as much on contemporary politics as on the past. To an Athenian audience, Ion's reluctance to participate in public life would not seem a pious focus on higher things, but a refusal to act as an adult male should. We see a similar portrayal in Euripides' *Hippolytus*, where Hippolytus' refusal to make the transition to adulthood is demonstrated not only by his hostility to marriage but also by his rejection of political participation (983-91).[4] The anxiety felt in any major transition is frequently expressed as a desire to avoid it: for example, Greek wedding poetry often suggests the fears felt by a bride as she leaves her status as a child, and a wish that she could remain in her old life.[5] Unlike Hippolytus, though, whose refusal to accept maturity results in his death, Ion comes to recognise the impossibility of remaining a youth and accepts the need to take on the responsibilities of an adult man.

Political identity: Athenians and foreigners

Ion's story also follows his discovery of an Athenian identity, and it is this heritage that proves essential in establishing his right to be adopted as Xouthos' son. Ion himself anticipates trouble as an outsider, and suggests that the Athenians will be hostile to his arrival (589-92) and that he will not enjoy the same rights as a true-born citizen:

'If a foreigner turns up in a city of pure blood, even if he is a citizen in theory, he has the voice of a slave and no freedom of speech.' (673-5)

The Chorus' hostility to Ion is characterised as deriving as much from the fact he is a foreigner as from their personal loyalty to Creousa. In their initial response to the adoption, they stress Xouthos' own status as a foreigner (703-4), and explain their hope for Ion's death by referring to their city's history (720-4). Their resentment at the prospect of rule by an outsider becomes still more marked in the third stasimon, where they describe Ion's adoption as an attack on the

Athenian ruling house, and repeatedly stress their antipathy to Ion ruling Athens. Creousa's murder attempt is thus depicted as a form of patriotic self-defence, an idea emphasised by the Athenian origins of the poison she uses (999-1003).

Ion's discovery of his true birth is surrounded in Athenian language and imagery. Creousa rejoices not only in the discovery of a son, but in the acquisition of an Athenian heir: 'The land has a king, Erechtheus is young again' (1464-5), and swears on the name of Athene that her story about Ion's birth is true (1478, 1528-31). The importance of Ion's nationality is finally stressed by the appearance of Athene herself, who, acting as the personification of the city, affirms his right to rule Athens: 'Since he is born from Erechtheus' line, it is right for him to rule my land' (1573-4).

We can thus see the play as a journey from ignorance to knowledge, culminating in Ion and Creousa's new self-awareness and possession of the truth. However, this movement is complicated by the fact that the play ends in deception as well as revelation. Ion cannot publicly claim his true identity: he and Creousa are required by the gods to maintain the lie. Athene's speech at the end of the play implies that Ion will be seamlessly integrated into Athens, yet logically the need to hide the truth ought to incur the same level of hostility that Ion originally feared. Just as the play upholds the importance of the blood-parent bond over the social aspects of parenting (see Chapter 3), so too *Ion* suggests that realities are more important than perceptions. At the end of the play, what matters is not that Ion is publicly proclaimed as the true-born heir to Athens, but that the bloodline is in fact continued. *Ion* suggests that the objective truth of heritage and bloodlines runs deeper than the social status attributed to them. Ion's own awareness of his true identity, and the divine approval conferred upon him because of it, nullify any further obstacles the rest of the world may present.[6]

Autochthony and the Erechtheid myth

The play's handling of its Athenian theme draws on contemporary ideas about citizenship and autochthony. Athenian myth stressed that Athenians were autochthonous: native to the land they inhabited.[7] Autochthony acts as a justification to rule over the land and an explanation of the people's connection to it. It suggests unity between the citizens, deriving from their common origin, and also implies that the city has peaceful origins: the right to inhabit it is a natural one, not achieved by force of conquest.[8] The concept of autochthony is embedded in the foundation myth of the ruling house, in which the original king, Erichthonius, is literally born from the earth. The house of the Erechtheids, therefore, is the ultimate symbol of Athenian autochthony, and the myth of their origins underlines their right to rule the land. Athenians are referred to as autochthonous throughout the play, and it is this word which Ion uses to anticipate Athenian hostility at his arrival: 'They say that the famous autochthonous Athenians are not a people brought in from outside the land' (589-90). Similarly, in Euripides' fragmentary play *Erechtheus,* Athenian autochthony is used as an argument for the city's superiority: immigrant communities are described as 'a peg fitted badly into a piece of wood', and called 'citizen in words alone, not in deeds' (fr. 360.7-12).

The importance of autochthony to Athenian self-definition can be seen by comparing it to the foundation myth for the Dorian peoples (including the Spartans and other Peloponnesians). The Dorians were believed to have accompanied the children of Heracles, who, driven out of their native land by the wicked king Eurystheus, invaded other Greek lands and expelled the native (Ionian) population.[9] The Ionian refugees crossed to the coast of Asia Minor, except for the Athenians who remained in Attica.[10] Dorian mythology thus allows its descendants to pride themselves on their military prowess: we find frequent references in Greek writers to the belief that the Dorians were militarily superior to the Ionians, whom they viewed as weak and effeminate.[11] Conversely, the focus for Ionian pride is their indigenous status, which makes them (in Ionian eyes) inherently superior to the immigrant Dorians.[12] Thus, the Athenian obsession with autochthony is a way of competing with rival cities and defusing their competing claims to superiority: autochthony is, as it were, the Athenians' Unique Selling Point.[13]

The Erechtheid myth is alluded to throughout *Ion*, beginning in Hermes' prologue, where the god mentions Creousa's Erechtheid heritage (10, 20-6). Upon meeting Creousa for the first time, Ion's first question is whether the myth of the family's origins is true (265-7), and he goes on to ask further about the history of the house (268-82). This series of questions reminds the audience of the myth, but also establishes it as important to the play. The Erechtheid connection is further stressed when Creousa and the old slave lay their plans for Ion's murder: the poison Creousa uses was given to Erichthonius by Athene immediately after his birth from the soil of Attica (999-1003). Creousa's inheritance of the poison and its encasement in a family heirloom highlights her own birthright, as well as the degree to which the Erechtheid story continues to influence the kingship of Athens.

The myth does not simply form a backdrop to the play's action; scholars have also noted how Ion's own story is presented as a re-enactment of the house's foundation myth.[14] Both Ion and Erichthonius are born in the wilderness (Ion in a cave, Erichthonius directly from the earth), rescued by a god (Hermes and Athene), and given to a foster-mother. The ornaments Creousa leaves in Ion's cradle, and which enable his identification, are said to recall Erichthonius' origins: the golden snakes symbolise the live snakes which Athene put on the baby to protect him, and Creousa calls them 'imitations of Erichthonius' (1429).

We find a further echo of the Erichthonius myth when Ion, frustrated by Xouthos' inability to tell him his mother's identity, suggests he must be born from the earth. Ion's comment is presumably meant as a sarcastic jibe, but Xouthos takes it seriously: 'the land does not beget children' (542). The importance of the myth in the play enhances the significance of this scene. Xouthos' apparent ignorance of it not only adds to the comic elements of his portrayal, but also feeds into the tensions that surround foreigners in Athens: as a non-Athenian, he fundamentally misunderstands the house he claims to represent. Ion, on the other hand, may intend the comment as a joke, but its effect is ironic. His suggestion that he was born from the ground reflects the assimilation of his own story to that of the Erechtheid house. His aside is truer than he knows.

The autochthony myth is not simply replicated as an uncomplicated piece of patriotism, however, and various scholars have noted the way that *Ion* explores the implications of autochthony. In particular, a problem which arises with assimilating Ion and Erichthonius is that autochthony is incompatible with maternity. As various scholars have noted, one function of an autochthony myth is to exclude women from the foundation of the city, for its founder is born directly from the earth.[15] According to myth, Erichthonius was born from the sperm of Hephaestus which fell on the soil of Attica following a failed attempt to seduce Athene, and while *Ion* does not directly allude to this story, we can assume the audience would have been familiar with it.[16] Athene herself was also motherless, and was born directly from the head of Zeus, as the Chorus recall when they ask her to grant Creousa a child. The Chorus invoke Athene as 'you who were brought to birth without labour pangs or the goddess of childbirth' (452-3), an image which is striking in the context of a prayer for fertility. In Aeschylus' *Eumenides*,

Athene rejects the rights of the mother precisely because of her own origins (733-6), and she is presented as having masculine traits throughout Greek literature.[17] The theme of autochthony, therefore, implies an effacing of the female, enhanced in *Ion* by the importance of Athene as another symbol of Athens.

One important difference between the Athenian autochthony myth and similar stories from other states is that Erichthonius is born a baby, rather than emerging from the earth as an adult man. As such, he is in need of nurture and protection, which is provided first by Athene and then by the daughters of Cecrops. The myth, therefore, recognises the need for female involvement, but it emphasises the roles women play as nurses and nurturers, rather than attributing importance to maternity itself.[18] We find a similar idea in Aeschylus' *Eumenides,* where Apollo argues that the mother's role in procreation is merely to act as container for the baby, and thus she does not have the same rights to the child's loyalty as the father (657-73). This division of the various functions of parenthood is, as we have seen, one of *Ion*'s most prominent themes. As we have already observed, however, the play ultimately upholds motherhood, and celebrates the bond between mother and child. The importance of motherhood, and the focus on Creousa, is thus in tension with the theme of autochthony.

Similarly, the Erechtheids are not the only figures described as earth-born in the play, for the adjective is used of other mythological creatures: the Giants and the Gorgon (987-9). For these destructive figures, being born from the earth emphasises their primitive and monstrous nature. They are placed in opposition to the gods, representing the clash of chaos with order. The battle of the gods and Giants was frequently used in religious iconography (for example on the east metopes of the Parthenon), and the Chorus allude to it in the *parodos,* when they see it portrayed in the sculptures at Delphi (206-11).[19] In the *parodos*, the Giants are set against Athene, who brandishes the head of the Gorgon against them, a symbol of dangerous forces subdued (209-11). This image is recalled as Creousa plots her revenge, when she describes not only 'the battle of the earth-born', but also Athene's killing of the Gorgon and acquisition of her skin for armour (987-98). The poison Creousa uses against Ion is a symbol of her Athenian and autochthonous origins, given to Erichthonius by Athene. But consisting as it does of the Gorgon's blood, it is also a symbol of the chaotic powers of earth. This double nature of the earth is encapsulated in the two drops of blood with their opposed powers: healing and death.[20] Ion himself uses autochthonous imagery to attack Creousa, and the earth imagery he invokes by calling her a snake and a Gorgon refers to her destructive side (1261-5). Thus, autochthony represents chaos as well as order, and monstrosity as well as legitimacy.

Creousa insists on the separation between these two aspects, saying of the drops of blood: '[I keep them] separately: good and evil do not mix' (1016). The play, however, suggests that she is wrong, for the good and bad aspects of autochthony are interwoven. Creousa's own noble inheritance is connected to the darker aspect of her family: the deaths caused by opening the casket of Erichthonius, and the killing of Erechtheus' daughters (272-4, 278). These murders are disturbing, but they are nevertheless described as essential for the survival of the city (278). The depiction of Cecrops on Xouthos' tent as having the tail of a snake (1163-4) also symbolises the combination of the two, for the snake represents his earthborn nature in both its aspects: legitimising and monstrous. Barbara Goff, who analyses the images in the tent, sees a broader pattern of order and chaos set in balance, and argues that the tent, the location for Ion's acceptance as an Athenian, symbolises Athenian identity in all its complexity.[21] Moreover we see a similar ambiguity in the image of the Gorgon. The Gorgon appears in the play as a poisonous monster (1015), but Ion also tells the Chorus that the sacred *omphalos*, the stone representing the navel of the earth and the heart of the sanctuary, is surrounded by images of Gorgons (224).[22] The sacred and the monstrous are inextricably linked, as symbolised by the conversion of the Gorgon's head into a divine weapon.

This exploration of potentially negative aspects of autochthony need not be understood as an attack on Athenian self-belief, but rather as a three-dimensional exploration of the tensions and conflicts involved in identity. As one scholar points out, there is an inherent strangeness in 'a drama about citizenship in which not a single character is a citizen, and in which it is the women who embody legitimacy and slaves who speak for the city ... in a word, a drama that tells of all the ways to be Athenian outside Athenian orthodoxy'.[23] These ways of being Athenian are presented as fundamentally positive and enriching, yet it is possible to misuse them. The prospect of violence inherent in the dark side of autochthony becomes actualised with Creousa's murder attempt, justified in terms of protecting the state from outsiders (1061-73). Just as Ion learns that the Gorgon is part of his own heritage as well as Creousa's, the play suggests a need to accept and seek a balance between the destructive and positive forces inherent in Athenian self-identity. This balance is embodied in the person of Athene, who is both the slayer of the Gorgon and the protector of Erichthonius.[24] Thus, the play's ending acknowledges the problems involved in autochthony (and by implication citizenship more generally) but suggests that they can be overcome.

Athens and empire

The Athenians' pride in their autochthonous roots needs to be balanced against the claim to a shared Ionian identity with the islanders that comprised their empire. These two beliefs are potentially incompatible, but *Ion* incorporates both, presenting the Athenian-born Ion as the founder of the Ionian race.[25] The play demonstrates Athens' right to rule its empire, both by right of birth and by divine will. Not only are the Athenians kin to the other Ionians, but they are their natural leaders, through Ion's original kingship. It is Athens' patron god Athene who announces Ion's Ionian future, and she proclaims it as part of his incorporation into the Athenian royal house (1572-88). Ion's own sons are given the names of the four original tribes of Athens (the Geleontes, Hopletes, Argades and Aigikores), and it is their descendants who go on to found the Ionian peoples. The tribes of Athens had been reorganised in 501, and their numbers were increased from four to ten. A contemporary audience would have been aware of the older system of four tribes, however, and Ion as father of these four becomes the direct ancestor of the Athenian people. Thus, Athenians and Ionians are presented as having a shared origin. Moreover, by giving Ion's sons the names of these tribes it is implied that the foundation of Ionia is something undertaken by the Athenian people as a whole, not simply by Ion as an individual.[26]

Throughout the fifth century, we see signs of discontent with the empire among various subject-cities. In 427, Mytilene had tried to revolt from the empire. In Thucydides' description of the debate in Athens over how to punish the Mytileneans, the speakers refer to the possibility of other cities revolting (3.39.7-8, 3.46.1-3): the implication is that many subject-cities are unhappy with the empire and will rebel if possible. As the Peloponnesian War progressed, Athens indeed faced increasing levels of revolt within the empire. Yet the empire was crucial to Athens' political and military survival: not only had it brought wealth and prestige, but more pragmatically it was allied tribute which funded the powerful Athenian navy. In addition, Athens depended on imported grain from the Black Sea, and control of the route to the Hellespont was essential in ensuring the corn-supply. Maintaining control of the empire was therefore vital: according to Thucydides, the exiled Athenian general Alcibiades advised the Spartans that severing Athens from her allies was one of the keys to winning the war (6.91.7). As Athens faced increasing levels of revolt in the late fifth century, there must have been internal anxiety as to whether she could maintain her empire. The celebration of the empire in a play at the Great Dionysia, an international festival whose rituals emphasised the bond between Athens and her subject-cities, therefore fulfils an obvious political function.[27]

Athene explains the settlement of Ionia as something which comes about in order to benefit Athens:

> 'At the fated time, the children born from [Ion's sons] will settle in the island cities of the Cyclades and the land on the coast, which will give strength to my land.' (1581-5).

Colonies were expected to remain loyal to their mother-cities, and so the implication is that providing Athens with assistance is the allies' duty.[28] As such, Athens' demands for tribute are justifiable, and allied cities which seek to leave the empire are rebelling against the claims of kinship and their divinely ordained destiny, as well as their sworn treaty obligations.

Patriotism and 'propaganda'

It is undeniable that a strong strand of Athenian self-belief runs through the play. As well as the frequent references to Athenian heritage and local myth, we also find explicit praise of the city. When Creousa introduces herself to Ion, he is struck with awe at her Athenian origins: 'You live in a famous city and are sprung from noble ancestors – how I marvel at you, my lady' (262-3). Ion as an outsider expresses surprise that Creousa has married a foreigner: he assumes her husband must be *eugenês* ('noble'), then asks how Xouthos could marry someone *engenês* ('born in the land'); the implication is that the two terms are interchangeable, and thus that simply being Athenian is equivalent to noble birth.[29] The Chorus consistently assert the splendour of Athens: indeed their opening lines express surprise and wonder at finding architectural beauty anywhere else: 'So it's not just in holy Athens that there are halls of the gods with lovely columns' (184-7). *Ion* was produced in the last years of the Peloponnesian War, at a time when Athens was facing tensions within the empire, and increasingly aware of her own unpopularity with her subject-cities. The foreshadowing of Athens' empire reminds the audience that Athenian greatness is divinely ordained, and smoothes over the fraught relationship between Athenians and islanders by stressing shared ties of kinship and heritage. *Ion* can therefore be read as a fairly unsubtle piece of Athenian self-assertion, designed to bolster Athens' image as leader as well as reflecting the Athenians' deep-seated belief in their own superiority.

Modern readers frequently find it difficult to respond to this aspect of *Ion*, and find a patriotic interpretation of the play disappointing. Influenced by the use of propaganda in twentieth-century dictatorships, we regard overt praise of the state with suspicion, and associate it with censorship and brainwashing. We also tend to assume that patriotic art is devoid of artistic merit, and view the role of literature as to challenge and subvert the establishment, rather than to uphold it. This kind of aesthetic preconception is a significant factor in the tendency in scholarship to problematise the patriotic aspect of *Ion*, and to read the praise of Athens and her empire as ironic, and so question the ultimate outcome of Athene's decrees.[30] In recent times, this line has been argued most influentially by Nicole Loraux, who writes of *Ion*: 'To believe that its lesson can be so easily grasped would be to forget that in Euripides' hands, tragedy involves a systematic distortion of all dominant values'.[31] If we take as a starting premise the idea that

Euripides always sets out to subvert and undermine the establishment, we can use it to justify ironic readings of *Ion*, or of any other Euripidean play. This kind of argument, however, is in severe danger of circularity, for it is only by reading the texts that we are able to draw conclusions about Euripides' political and moral outlook.

In order to understand Greek tragedy in its original context, we must attempt to read it through the values of its own time, and not through our aesthetic assumptions. Terms such as 'propaganda' are misleading, firstly because of their inherently negative connotations, and secondly because they suggest intentional control and manipulation by the state.[32] The City Dionysia may be a state-run festival, but it is hardly a Stalinist event: the most powerful factor governing playwrights was the desire to write a successful piece, not the need to comply with government regulations. Referring to patriotic passages as 'propaganda' implies that the Athenian *polis* had to foist such views upon its audience, and that these views do not reflect the attitudes of the average audience member. We should treat this assumption with enormous care: to a modern audience, patriotism is somewhat embarrassing, but to an ancient one it was a straightforward matter. Loyalty to the *polis* was a standard part of Greek values, and we find it expressed throughout Greek literature.[33] For example, in Solon's account of the ideal life in Herodotus, it is significant that Tellus the Athenian dies fighting for his country, a fate which is described as 'a glorious death' (1.30.21-5).

We should also note that tragedy consistently portrays Athens in a positive light. Athens is never the location for plays depicting the catastrophic fall of a royal house or noble individual: these distressing events take place in other cities. Instead, Athens is frequently presented as a place which can provide salvation and resolution for fallen heroes from other states. Athens takes in suppliants and exiles, and offers them sanctuary and purification (for example, Aeschylus' *Eumenides*; Sophocles' *Oedipus at Colonus*). Athens also fights for the rights of the weak and the oppressed, against opponents who represent tyranny (Euripides' *Children of Heracles, Suppliant Women*). Athenian kings tend to be wise and socially-minded (for example, Theseus in *Oedipus at Colonus*, or Euripides' *Suppliant Women*), rather than the flawed and egotistical rulers we see depicted elsewhere. When Athenian rulers do behave less than perfectly, they do so when they are temporarily away from Athens, thus distancing them from the city (for example, Aegeus in *Medea* is passing through Corinth; Theseus in *Hippolytus* is at Troezen).[34] If tragedy is normally distanced from the audience's world in terms of time and space, a play with a strong Athenian connection removes one of those elements. It is not appropriate to criticise Athens, even mythological Athens, in a civic festival designed to show the city at its best.

In this context, Ion's acquisition of an Athenian identity is presented as a straightforward good and a compensation for his earlier loneliness. The supremacy of Athenian nationality is alluded to throughout the play, beginning with Ion's admiring comments to Creousa when they first meet. It is also true that the play scrutinises the morality of Apollo's actions, but it does not follow that Ion's own destiny is tainted as a result. Creousa may rail against her rape by Apollo, but she also regrets the loss of the baby and rejoices in the arrival of an heir to the Erechtheid throne. The end of the play acknowledges Apollo's embarrassment (1557-8), but also rejoices in the divine heritage granted to Athens (1488): there is no implication of incompatibility between the two.

This is not to suggest that *Ion's* presentation of Athens is simply jingoistic flag-waving, or that it serves no purpose other than to flatter the audience by reminding them of their superiority to all other nations. As we have already seen, *Ion* alludes to dark episodes in Athenian history such as the murder of Erechtheus' daughters (Creousa's sisters), while nevertheless praising the city. The death of Erechtheus' daughters is horrific, but is carried out for the greater good and for the protection of the community (278). Euripides expands upon this idea in his *Erechtheus*, where the deaths form the play's central action. The emotional core of *Erechtheus* is the personal cost to the girls and their parents of this sacrifice, yet the play affirms the importance of the community, and suggests that it is the individual's duty to put him or herself at its service: indeed in this version only one death is required, and the other girls voluntarily offer up their lives in addition in solidarity with their sister's heroism. The largest surviving fragment is a speech by Praxithea, the girls' mother, where she accepts her daughter must die, and argues for the supreme importance of self-sacrifice to ensure the state's survival (fr. 360). The play is effective precisely because the deaths are serious and emotionally engaging: it would not be dramatically powerful if the audience were expected to respond with uncomplicated enthusiasm to the sacrifices. But the greatness of the cost enhances the nobility of the sacrifice, and hence casts greater glory upon the community for whose benefit it was made. Praxithea's speech survives because it was quoted by the fourth-century orator Lycurgus as an example of female heroism (*Against Leocrates* 100). Lycurgus' approval confirms that we are meant to admire Praxithea, but also to appreciate the enormity of the sacrifice she is making. Ion's own story is analogous. The human cost is acknowledged, and we are required to engage fully with Ion and Creousa's suffering in order to appreciate the play. Nonetheless, this suffering does not detract from the glory of Ion's Athenian future, any more than Ion's awareness of the Erechtheids' deaths taints his admiration for Athens. Just as autochthony has a monstrous as well as a noble aspect, the play recognises the human sacrifices that underpin great achievements. But this recognition glorifies the ultimate outcome, rather than undermining it. Athenian identity can be presented in a way which is positive but still three-dimensional. However, such concern about the play's pro-Athenian tone runs deeper than simply tying into a modern dislike for patriotic literature. It is also related to the wider issue of how we should respond to *Ion*'s apparently happy ending, and it is this issue which we will address in the final chapter.

Happy Endings?

Ion's optimistic ending and upbeat tone has frequently been a source of anxiety for modern readers. The play has often been described as a 'tragicomedy' or 'romantic comedy' by critics who feel uncomfortable classing a piece with a happy ending as a tragedy. More recently, a common line of scholarship has been to downplay the 'romantic' and 'comic' elements in the play, and to argue for a darker subtext to the apparently cheerful ending. This chapter will discuss the strengths and limitations of both these approaches, and examine questions of genre within tragedy. In the light of the earlier analysis of the play's themes, we can attempt to assess how we should respond to the ending, and how seriously *Ion* is to be taken.

Ion as 'tragicomedy'

Twentieth-century scholarship frequently invented terms such as 'tragicomedy', 'romance', or 'melodrama' to describe *Ion* and other Euripidean plays similar in tone and content.[1] The use of such vocabulary presupposes that these plays do not fit adequately into the category of 'tragedy', and that describing them as 'tragic' is in some sense misleading. Part of the problem is a linguistic one: a modern English reader's understanding of tragedy is conditioned not only by the popular use of the word to mean 'very sad event', but also by the adoption of the term to describe later drama. Thus it is tempting to read our understanding of 'tragedy', influenced by Shakespearian and Jacobean tragedy, back into an ancient text and then to problematise the differences we find between the play and our expectations. However, another part of the problem these critics find in classing *Ion* as a tragedy is the striking difference in tone and moral message from darker and more 'conventional' tragedies such as *Medea* or *Oedipus the King*. *Ion* reverses the structure of these tragedies in that the play depicts a movement from sorrow to joy, and ends in harmony rather than catastrophe. Both the main characters are better off than at the start of the play, and the gods act to protect the human characters from their fallible mortal instincts.

Furthermore, these features of *Ion* are also reminiscent of New Comedy, the dominant form of comic drama in the fourth-century BC. In contrast to Old Comedy, which used fantastical situations as a setting for political and social satire, New Comedy was set in a realistic world and was based on the lives of ordinary people, drawn from a range of stock characters. The plots focus around love-affairs, lost or abandoned children, and mistaken identities, and the plays frequently end with a revelation which removes the obstacles to the hero's happiness. The similarities between *Ion* and New Comedy are highlighted by the survival of a play by Menander titled 'The Arbitration' (*Epitrepontes*). The play opens with an estranged marriage: the husband (Charisios) has discovered that his wife (Pamphile) produced a baby a mere five months after their marriage, and has left home to drown his sorrows in drinking and sex. Meanwhile, the baby, which was exposed by the wife, has been found by a shepherd and adopted by a charcoal-burner whose own baby had recently died. The two men argue over the possession of some trinkets found along with the baby, and in the arbitration scene which gives the play its title, it is decided that the ornaments should stay with the child. These trinkets lead to the child's identification, as the ring left with it turns out to belong to Charisios, the estranged husband. It then emerges that Charisios raped Pamphile, who later became his wife, at a festival, unaware of her identity. The baby's legitimate status is therefore assured, and the couple are happily reunited.

The similarities with *Ion* in terms of theme and plot-devices are striking: a rape which is later smoothed over, an abandoned child and distressed mother, issues of legitimacy ultimately settled by foundling tokens. These individual components are also found in other New Comedy plays, which frequently hinge around a child lost or abandoned at birth, or a woman whose virtue is questioned.[2] However, these similarities need to be handled with care. New Comedy does indeed confirm that certain features of *Ion* (and other late Euripidean tragedy) were viewed as potentially light-hearted by an ancient audience, because of their later adoption into comic plays. What it does not confirm, however, is that *Ion* was intended to play the role of a comedy rather than a tragedy. Euripides' own understanding of comedy would be based on the political plays of Aristophanes: comedy of character and situation did not exist in his day. Labels such as 'tragicomedy' presuppose an intentional difference between *Ion* and a 'pure' tragedy, which in turn is based on the assumption that Euripides and his audience knew of a form of comedy which in fact only developed in the following century.[3] We should instead recognise the influence that runs in the opposite direction: the poets of New Comedy were influenced by tragedy as much as by Old Comedy in devising a new form of drama.[4]

We should also not overlook the traditional elements of *Ion*'s plot. Stories of abandoned babies and the later discovery of their true identities are a conventional element of Greek myth. These babies are usually of royal or divine birth; they are often given supernatural protection while in the wild, and are raised in humble circumstances.[5] For example, Zeus himself is hidden away as a baby, and raised by nymphs and by a magical goat.[6] While the abandonment myth frequently has a happy ending, it is not automatically light or humorous. In the Trojan myth cycle, Paris is abandoned as a baby and raised as a shepherd, but his survival leads to the destruction of his city. The story of Oedipus is, in structural terms, not dissimilar to the plots of *Ion* or indeed of New Comedy: the baby is exposed, protected by divine fate, and discovered by a kindly mortal; its identity is later uncovered by analysing the circumstances under which it was found. The difference, of course, is that Oedipus' discovery of his true birth is a source of horror, and brings about the destruction rather than the salvation of the family unit. Nevertheless, both plays draw on the same mythological theme. Herodotus presents similar stories in his *Histories*: for example his description of the birth of Cyrus, the first and greatest of the Persian Kings (1.107-16). Cyrus too is born under inauspicious circumstances, which lead to his exposure (the King has been warned that if his daughter gives birth, the child will usurp the throne). The baby is believed to be dead, but is in fact spared and brought up by a kindly herdsman. His identity is then revealed as a boy because he cannot hide his intrinsic nobility, so is revealed as more than the son of a slave. Herodotus also refers to a previous and more fantastic version of the story, where Cyrus is miraculously saved by supernatural forces, and is suckled by a bitch in the mountains (1.122). Exposure stories are not limited to Greek culture, but are found in the myths of other Indo-European peoples: for example, the story of Moses, or of Romulus and Remus. The foundling who turns out to have a special destiny still has a grip over the modern imagination, as demonstrated by characters from popular art such as Superman, Luke Skywalker, and Harry Potter. Thus, in composing the plot of *Ion*, Euripides is drawing on a traditional story-pattern with which his audience would have been familiar. The prevalence of this motif in New Comedy, and later in Roman Comedy, does not imply an association with the comic genre, but rather confirms the lasting power of this story-pattern.

If we wish to query the 'tragicomedy' label, we need to look at *Ion*'s relationship to other models of tragedy.[7] It is easy to see why scholars perceive *Ion* to be unusual because of its happy ending. In addition, *Ion* has obvious similarities with certain other plays by Euripides, hence the temptation to create a sub-category: *Alcestis*, *Helen*, and *Iphigeneia Among the Taurians* have similarly optimistic endings. Like *Ion*, the plots of these plays focus on the reunion of a family and the re-establishment of normal relationships, and contain an element of abandonment or loss, and of mistaken identity. All four plays show a wider movement from chaos to order, and from suffering to happiness. Finally, *Ion* also contains various episodes which are often regarded as having a 'light' or 'comic' tone: for example, the misunderstandings in the recognition scene between Ion and Xouthos; the characterisation of Xouthos as foolish and gullible; the 'everyday' tone set by Ion's performance of his temple duties in his opening monody; and the way the Chorus behave like tourists in the *parodos*.[8]

However, marking out *Ion* (and other similar plays) as belonging to a special category makes it easy to overlook the similarities between *Ion* and more conventionally 'tragic' plays. Many tragedies end on a note of optimism: for example Aeschylus' *Eumenides* or Sophocles' *Philoctetes*. Other tragedies also contain moments of humour, or scenes where the tone is lighter. For example, when Orestes' old Nurse in *Libation Bearers* recalls how he vomited and shat as a baby, it is hard not to see this as a deliberate contrast with the high-flown style and bleak tone of the surrounding material (753-60). Similarly, Euripides' *Orestes* includes a singing Phrygian eunuch at a moment of tension as we wait to learn whether Helen has been murdered (1369-1502). It is fair to argue that

Euripides made more sustained use of lighter moments than the other two tragedians, but he does so in plays whose grim endings are undisputable. For example, *Bacchae* contains a humorous depiction of two old men trying to dance for Dionysus like young girls (170-209). We might also point to parallels in Shakespearian tragedy: for example the Porter's speech in *Macbeth* comes at a bleak moment in the play, but is filled with undeniably bawdy and comic elements (2.3.1-22), while the Gravedigger scene in *Hamlet* contains witty banter between the two gravedigger-clowns, whom the eponymous hero also engages in wordplay (5.1.1-183). We are not reluctant to classify *Hamlet* or *Macbeth* as tragedies despite both plays containing moments which rely on humour to achieve their desired effect. Yet when it comes to Greek tragedy, scholars frequently feel uncomfortable allowing the genre a similar level of flexibility.

The discomfort with 'happy' tragedies originates partly from modern conceptions of 'the tragic', influenced by anachronistic assumptions about Greek theatre. To today's audience, 'tragedy' means something quite specific in terms of overall plot-arc and ultimate resolution. It is easy to forget that in the fifth century BC, theatre had only two genres, tragedy and (old) comedy, and thus that tragedy encompassed a far broader range of material and themes than we might at first suppose. To a fifth-century audience, on the other hand, 'comic' would have meant Old Comedy, and the 'comic' elements in *Ion* and other tragedies are very different from anything we find in Aristophanes. The status of these plays as tragedies, therefore, is unaffected by variations in mood and tone, or even moments of deliberate humour.

There is also a noticeable tendency among scholars of tragedy to look for 'rules' for the genre. This originates in the writing of Aristotle, who attempts to define the formal features of tragedy in his *Poetics*.[9] Aristotle's conception of tragedy is that it is based around the fall of a great man through self-

91

willed action, and he takes *Oedipus the King* as his example of a perfect tragedy. Whilst Aristotle's observations are not without their merits, it is important to remember that he is a literary critic, writing about a century after the original performance context; as such his theories have no more privileged authority than those of any other reader or audience member.

One further factor we should take care not to overlook is that the tragedies that have survived into our age have not done so by chance. All the surviving works by Sophocles and Aeschylus and many of the plays by Euripides were selected by later generations on the basis that they were the finest, or the best to teach to school children. These plays were copied onto papyri and later medieval manuscripts, and happened to survive into the modern era. We know little about the process by which plays were selected, but it seems likely that the scholars and teachers making such choices were biased by their own preconceptions about tragedy, and were very likely influenced by Aristotle's preference for unhappy endings. Fortunately, we also have a small number of randomly selected plays, because of the survival of a manuscript containing nine plays of Euripides, arranged in alphabetical order (covering the Greek letters eta to kappa).[10] Compared to the select plays, a far higher proportion of these 'non-select' plays (which include *Ion*) are optimistic in tone.[11] It therefore seems highly likely that tragedies with upbeat endings were perfectly normal in the Greek world. Indeed, judging by the statistical evidence, it even seems plausible to suggest that 'tragic' plays (i.e. those with catastrophic outcomes) were in the minority.

In terms of laying down rules about tragedy, therefore, we must provide sufficiently broad scope that any play in the surviving *corpus* is included. We can begin by making certain observations about what distinguished tragedy from comedy to a fifth-century Greek.

Tragedy is usually set in the mythological world, and has no

explicit contemporary references; it makes little or no reference to its own theatricality, and the poet never steps outside
the dramatic world in order to address the audience directly.
The tragic world is 'realistic' in a way that the comic one is
not: while we may get the gods, monsters, and heroes with
miraculous powers of traditional myth, the tragic world is
bound by the rules of this established mythological universe.
We do not find free-form fantasy or absurdist situations
dramatised on stage as we do in Aristophanes. Most impor-
tantly, however, tragedy contains serious content, and depicts
human suffering.[12]

Whether or not *Ion* ends happily, in order to appreciate the
play we are required to empathise with Creousa's suffering.
The happy ending is compensation for the earlier pain the
human characters have experienced; as such, to enjoy the
ending fully we must acknowledge the full extent of their
earlier ordeals. In contrast, when comic characters suffer, we
are invited to laugh at them, and nothing provokes us to experience their suffering as real or meaningful. Tragedy explores
issues of contemporary concern, and the events we see on stage
are often painful and disturbing. We frequently see the breakdown of social order and inter-personal relationships. While the
conflicts that tragic characters face are similar to those an audience member might face in his own life (how to behave towards
one's family, how to live in a community), the scale of both the
dilemma and its consequences is extreme. What matters, therefore, is not the ultimate outcome of these issues, and whether
the plays end in bleak despair or with a glimmer of optimism.
Rather, it is important that tragedy gives meaning to everyday
human concerns by its exploration of them, and that it exam-
ines these issues in a serious way.

Returning to *Ion*, it is indisputable that the play contains
serious ideas. The play's emotional focus lies in Creousa's
distress at her rape and at the loss of her child. While the

ending of the play encourages us to recognise the compensation that has now been given to her, this does not mean that her earlier suffering is not taken seriously. As we have seen in previous chapters, the play also tackles themes of social and intellectual importance. We find an exploration of what it means to be Athenian, the relationship between parent and child, and the nature of the gods. The fact that the play ends on an optimistic note does not lessen the impact of the ideas it has presented. The philosophical and moral discussions of *Ion* are treated seriously within the context of the play, and the fact that events turn out well for the mortal characters does not prevent the audience from reflecting upon the events they have observed.

Ironic *Ion*?

A more recent approach to *Ion* is to accept the seriousness of the play, but question the happy ending. Modern scholars suggest that the play encourages us to challenge the upbeat tone of the ending and to wonder whether the outcome is really as simple as Athene claims.[13] Critics who take this line point to Apollo's refusal to appear in person, and his admission of shame over his previous behaviour (1557-8). This creates a jarring effect in the play's final moments, which (they argue) calls into question the means by which the Ionians have acquired divine ancestry.[14] This veiled reference to Creousa's rape also reminds us of her earlier suffering, which (it is argued) casts doubt on the joyful tone of the ending. Thus, modern readers feel reluctant to lay aside the wrongs done to Creousa, or to accept that the sudden presentation of a son is adequate compensation for the past. A further troubling element is the continued deception of Xouthos, which contaminates the tone of revelation at the end of the play with a note of continued secrecy and deceit.

To an extent, this discussion comes down to questions of tone, which are largely subjective. For example, when Athene states 'Apollo has done everything well' (1595), and explains that Apollo granted Creousa a safe delivery and then protected his son, we could either read this as a straightforward explanation of the god's ultimate beneficence, or take it to be unnecessarily defensive, and note the incongruity with Apollo's reluctance to appear in person. However, we can attempt to reach a more conclusive answer to these questions by looking at the text in detail, and by analysing the issues it raises in the context of Greek popular morality.

Let us begin with the rape. The first pitfall to avoid is the problem of anachronism. Distasteful as it may seem to a modern reader, rape was simply not viewed in the same moral light in ancient Greek times as it is today. Rape was a crime, but was regarded less seriously than adultery, as the latter was felt to imply the moral corruption of the woman as well as the violation of her chastity.[15] A comparison with the plays of Menander helps us expose the fallacy that a play where the rapist goes unpunished cannot be regarded as having a happy ending.[16] Menander frequently uses rape as a plot-device, because it allows extra-marital sex to take place in a way that does not make us question the moral standards of the woman in question. In *Epitrepontes*, the discovery of the rape is central to resolving the misunderstandings and complications of the plot. To a modern audience, the plot-twist whereby Pamphile turns out to have been raped by the man who later became her husband is an extremely dark one. To Menander's audience, however, it appears to be no obstacle to the play's cheerful tone. Indeed, it is the discovery that Pamphile was raped rather than committing adultery which establishes her good moral character and hence allows for her reunion with her husband. We might exclaim over the double-standards which allow Charisios to rape a girl at a festival yet to condemn his wife for adulterous behaviour, and indeed Charisios himself acknowledges this hypocrisy at the end of the play (908-31). Yet the whole tone of *Epitrepontes* is cheerful, and the irony of these double-standards is presented in a wry tone, rather than in a way which seriously challenges or condemns the (male-dominated) social norms.

The difference with *Ion*, however, is that Euripides makes a point of presenting the rape as something dark and problematic by depicting Creousa's distress. Creousa's monody presents her pain in powerful terms, which mean that we cannot simply read the rape as a convenient plot-device. Nevertheless, the Greek audience is still less likely to be abidingly troubled by the rape than we are today. Presenting the rape as a morally outrageous event is Euripides' innovation, rather than the ethical *status quo*. As such, while the ancient audience is encouraged to take Creousa's suffering seriously, they lack our belief that rape is a horrific and psychologically scarring event, and thus would find it easier to accept the way Creousa's earlier pain is smoothed over at the end of the play (1609-12). In addition, we should not forget that the divine rape story was a familiar (and morally unproblematic) *topos* of Greek myth. Even though *Ion* deliberately complicates this theme, the audience's existing assumption that divine rape is a normal and positive part of myth makes it easier for them, along with Creousa, to make the transition to regarding the play's ending as a happy one.

Another important factor in annulling the dramatic effects of Creousa's monody is that her suffering is presented as connected to her loss of the baby: while the rape itself is independently condemned as bad behaviour, it is always spoken of in conjunction with the child's death and Apollo's failure to meet his obligations to mother and baby (338-48, 384-9, 437-9, 891-920, 939-52). This explains the dramatic change in tone when Creousa discovers her lost son. Even though logically the rape and Apollo's abandonment of the baby are unconnected, the presentation of the two as linked throughout the play means that it makes emotional sense that when one is disproved, the other ceases to be important any more. We should take Creousa's forgiveness of Apollo seriously as evidence: if it is Creousa's presentation of the rape that makes it morally problematic in the first place, her decision to let her grudge go at the end of the play should also guide our response.

We can make a similar case as regards Apollo's non-appearance. As we have already seen, his admission of shame is unconventional, and is part of the way that the play explores the differences between gods and men. The play's ending draws attention to Apollo's failure to assert his authority, rather than trying to downplay his absence, and this is used for dramatic effect. However, portraying Apollo as concerned with what humans think of him is used to highlight the absurdity of supposing that the gods can be held to mortal standards. As we have seen, the way *Ion* presents religion assumes that the audience knows that literature traditionally upholds a gulf between gods and men, and also engages with contemporary intellectual debate about this issue. The ending of *Ion* pokes fun at those philosophers who maintain the gods ought to be morally accountable. Apollo's embarrassment at facing a woman and an adolescent boy is certainly striking, but it is too absurd to be truly worrying.

Finally, to read the deception of Xouthos as problematic relies on the assumption that the audience feels sufficient sympathy with him that they are disturbed when Athene insists on the need to lie to him (1601-3). We should bear in mind that Xouthos has been presented in a humorous light: his main role is to form the comic foil to Ion's sincerity. We can also recall that Xouthos himself intended to deceive his wife in order to avoid upsetting her (657-8), and therefore only get what he deserves when the tables are turned. While not an unpleasant character, Xouthos is presented as foolish and thoughtless. What is most marked in his characterisation is his insensitivity to the feelings and concerns of the other characters: he fails to understand Ion's hesitation to leave his old life, or his desire to find his mother; he seriously underestimates the ease of persuading Creousa to accept his illegitimate son; and he misjudges the loyalties of the Chorus both as women and as Athenians. It is therefore largely *his* errors of judgment that have led to the near-disasters of the play's second half, which in turn adds to his characterisation as a buffoon. It seems unlikely, then, that the audience will feel particular concern for his dignity.[17] The deception of Xouthos is, as we have seen (Chapter 2), in logical terms unnecessary, for by literary convention Xouthos should accept Apollo's son into his house without concern. However, to preserve the play's conceit that the mortal characters really do regard the gods as being just like them, it is essential that Xouthos should not be easily persuaded. Treating Xouthos like a typical cuckold enhances the humorous aspect of his character, but it is also central to the play's religious and moral stance.

In conclusion, when considering ironic readings of *Ion*, it is important to bear in mind our own preconceptions about tragedy and about literature more generally. Like Aristotle, modern readers are conditioned to prefer tragedies with unhappy endings, and it is easy to assume that this kind of play is more likely to be 'deep' or 'meaningful' than a play which ends by resolving the problems it has raised. We also need to be careful that we do not read the text through the filter of our own cultural and moral suppositions (for example that rape is a terrible sexual crime, and that it causes psychological scarring which cannot be easily removed, or that empire is a source of guilt).

The Greeks expected poetry to contain a moral message, and the poet's role was perceived as a civic one. Aristophanes' comedy *Frogs* depicts a contest between Euripides and

Aeschylus as to which is the greater poet, and one of the factors considered is what moral and practical advice they give to the audience (1417-21). The interlocutors in Plato's dialogues frequently cite poets in order to justify or defend a particular viewpoint, and Plato's *Republic* contains a lengthy attack on poetry for propagating the wrong sort of morals.[18] We also know that it was considered inappropriate for tragedy to contain a message that was too overtly critical: Herodotus tells us that when the tragic poet Phrynichus put on a play about the sack of Miletus by the Persians in 493 (when the Athenians had not helped the Milesians), he was given a large fine for 'reminding them of their own troubles', and the play's reperformance was forbidden (6.21).

As we have seen, it is difficult to find clear support for an ironic reading of the play's patriotic tone in the text itself. Scholars who regard *Ion* as ironic tend to do so because of their belief that Euripides' work is fundamentally subversive and critical of Athenian norms.[19] However, as we have seen in the discussions of religion and family in the play, this is not a given, and it is just as natural to read the play as affirming everyday norms and values. It is true that the play does not trivialise the suffering of Ion and Creousa: we are led to understand how the events of the past have hurt both of them, and to recognise the extent of the damage done. Nevertheless, the play ends with the suggestion that it is possible to achieve harmony and joy despite past griefs, symbolised by Creousa's putting aside her resentment of Apollo.

Both of the readings of *Ion* discussed in this chapter share an underlying premise: they arise from discomfort that a play can both qualify as a tragedy and also end in a way which is sincerely optimistic. One school of thought seeks to resolve this problem by disqualifying *Ion* from being a tragedy in any meaningful sense of the term; the other tries to undermine the optimism of the ending. In this chapter, I have argued that both these approaches are misguided: we are wrong to problematise *Ion*'s happy ending, and the fact that we do so is based more on our own preconceptions and concerns than on a reading of the play or of Greek tragedy more generally. Acknowledging *Ion*'s fundamental optimism does not bind us into rejecting serious themes or concerns in the play. *Ion* explores various issues of contemporary concern, such as marriage, parenthood, identity, and religion, and the events we see on stage are often painful and disturbing as well as hopeful and humorous. While the problems Ion and Creousa face are more extreme than anything in the life of an ordinary Athenian, the underlying issues are of immediate importance to the ancient audience. It is often noted that tragedy, set in the mythological past, provides a safe forum in which to explore social norms, and question human behaviour. It does not follow, however, that the only worthwhile outcome to this process of exploration is the subversion of these norms. In *Ion,* we see the breakdown of social order and interpersonal relationships, but we also see their ultimate restoration. The optimism the play offers is one which recognises the cost of human suffering, but affirms its importance, and its capacity to achieve a greater good. The triumph of good at the end of *Ion* does not diminish the possibility of evil in human life, but the play's ending is sincere in its praise of family, religion, and city-state.

Notes

1. Play and Myth

1. Divine rapes occur frequently in myth and are often the source of heroic offspring, for example Danae and Leda were raped by Zeus, to produce Perseus and Helen respectively. The *topos* is sometimes inverted when a mortal man has intercourse with a goddess, for example Peleus and Thetis (parents of Achilles); Anchises and Aphrodite (parents of Aeneas).

2. For the ancient sources, see Hesiod fr. 9, 10.20-3 MW; Herodotus 5.66.2, 7.94.1, 8.44.2; Pausanias 7.1.2-5.

3. See D.J. Conacher, *Euripidean Drama: Myth, Theme and Structure* (Toronto, 1967) 271.

4. The Archive of Performances of Greek and Roman Drama Database (www.apgrd.ox.ac.uk) lists 58 perfomances based on *Ion* between 1754 and 2005. In comparison, the archive lists 634 performances based on *Medea*, 737 on Aeschylus' *Agamemnon*, and 686 on Sophocles' *Oedipus the King*.

5. A. Dacier, *La Poétique d'Aristote: traduite en français avec des remarques d'André Dacier* (Paris, 1692) 222.

6. There had in fact been a French opera in 1712 entitled *Créuse l'Athénienne*, based on Euripides' *Ion*, but there is no evidence to suggest Whitehead was influenced by it in writing his stage version.

7. See E. Hall and F. Macintosh, *Greek Tragedy and the British Theatre, 1660-1914* (Oxford, 2005) 128-251.

8. G. Reichard, *August Wilhelm Schlegels 'Ion': Das Schauspiel und die Aufführungen unter der Leitung von Goethe und Iffland* (Bonn, 1987) gives a history of the play's original performance and negative reception. Part of the reason for the play's unpopularity was that contemporary audiences found the portrayal of Creousa's rape immoral.

9. Hall and Macintosh (n. 7) 282-303.

10. A.W. Verrall, *Euripides the Rationalist: a Study in the History of Art and Religion* (Cambridge, 1895) 138-76.

11. E.R. Dodds, 'Euripides the Irrationalist (A Paper Read before the Classical Association, April 12, 1929)', *CR* 43(3) (1929) 97-104 at 97.

12. See E. Gregory, *H.D. and Hellenism: Classic Lines* (Cambridge, 1997) 205-18 for an analysis of H.D.'s *Ion*.

13. *Swallow Song* was originally performed in the Getty Centre, Los Angeles (October 2004). *Seven Pomegranate Seeds* was commissioned to launch the Onassis Programme for the Performance of Greek Drama in Oxford (May 2006).

14. Param Vir's *Ion* was first performed at the Aldeburgh Festival in 2000. The first full production was a co-production between Music Theatre Wales, Opéra national du Rhin and the Berliner Festwochen. Reviewers criticised the wordiness of the libretto, and its attempt to include wordplay and irony. See *Observer*, 2 November 2003 (http://observer.guardian.co.uk/review/story/0,,1075754,00.html); *The Times*, 25 October 2003 (http://entertainment.timesonline.co.uk/tol/arts_and_entertainment/article1000886.ece).

2. Tragedy and its Contexts

1. See A.W. Pickard-Cambridge, *The Dramatic Festivals of Athens* (Oxford, 1988) 57-101 and E. Csapo and W.J. Slater, *The Context of Ancient Drama* (Ann Arbor, 1995) 103-21 for a detailed account of the City Dionysia.

2. At *Frogs* 1110-18, the Chorus urge Aeschylus and Euripides to rely on the Athenian audience's sophistication, analytical skills, and detailed knowledge of the corpus of tragedy. While it is unlikely that the average audience member actually had the level of familiarity with the plays implied by the passage, it is nonetheless telling that Aristophanes thinks it a worthwhile strategy to flatter the audience by suggesting that they did.

3. The task of funding a play was allocated to the richest citizens every year, along with various other civic responsibilities (such as funding an athletic team or a warship). Being the funder (*chorêgos*) was a significant financial burden, but could also be used to win admiration and respect from the populace. In court, wealthy defendants often use their commitment as a *chorêgos* to establish their good character and dedication to the city (e.g. Lysias *Defence Against a Charge of Bribery* 1-5; Isaeus *Estate of Apollodorus* 38; Antiphon *On the Choreut* 11-13). For a detailed account of the choregic system, see P.

Wilson, *The Athenian Institution of the Khoregia: the Chorus, the City, and the Stage* (Cambridge, 2000).

4. Thucydides 1.89-117 and Plutarch *Life of Pericles* give an account of the process by which the Athenians assumed power. For a modern discussion, see P.A. Brunt, 'The Hellenic League Against Persia', *Historia* 2 (1953) 135-63; R. Sealey, 'The Origin of the Delian League', in E. Badian (ed.) *Ancient Society and Institutions* (Oxford, 1966) 233-55; R. Meiggs, *The Athenian Empire* (Oxford, 1972) 42-9.

5. After its attempt to revolt from the League was put down in 446/5 (M-L 52), Chalcis is made to swear to obey the Athenian *dêmos*. A similar settlement made with Erythrae in 453/2 (M-L 40) had stipulated obedience to the allies as well as to Athens, suggesting that Athens was becoming increasingly imperialistic in the intervening years. Similarly, the Erythrae decree refers to the League as an alliance ('*summachis*'), rather than 'the cities which the Athenians control'. See, however, P. Low, 'Looking for the Language of Athenian Imperialism', *JHS* 125 (2005) 93-111 for a discussion of whether this type of language was felt to be as brutal as modern scholars sometimes take it to be.

6. At Thucydides 3.47, Diodotus argues against punishing the democratic faction in Mytilene on the grounds that it will encourage democratic factions in other subject-cities, who currently support Athens, to turn against her and thus increase the level of revolt in the empire.

7. See K. Zacharia, *Converging Truths: Euripides' Ion and the Athenian Quest for Self-Definition* (Leiden, 2003) 50-5 on the manipulation of ethnicity within Athens and Ionia.

8. See Thucydides 3.86, 6.6, 6.76.

9. J.J. Coulton, *The Architectural Development of the Greek Stoa* (Oxford, 1976) 39, 99 and J. Walsh, 'The Date of the Athenian Stoa at Delphi', *AJA* 90 (1986) 319-36 at 333-4 argue that the Athenian stoa at Delphi is a statement of Athens' alliance with the Ionian Greeks, while J. Onians, *Bearers of Meaning: the Classical Orders in Antiquity, the Middle Ages, and the Renaissance* (Princeton, 1988) 15-18 also suggests that the temple of Athene at Cape Sunium reflects Athens' political leanings. See, however, E.P. McGowan, 'The Origins of the Athenian Ionic Capital', *Hesperia* 66 (1997) 209-33 who argues (n. 99) that the increasing use of the Ionic order was more to do with individual change in taste and artistic commissions than part of a political programme.

10. See S. Goldhill, 'The Great Dionysia and Civic Ideology', in J.J. Winkler and F.I. Zeitlin (eds) *Nothing to do with Dionysos? Athenian Drama in its Social Context* (Princeton, 1990) 97-129 for a discussion of the festival's ideological overtones.

11. Our information about dramatic victories comes mainly from official inscriptions, compilations by ancient scholars, and fragments from victory monuments erected for successful entries. See Pickard-Cambridge (n. 1) 70-4. Euripides won a fifth victory posthumously, with a production including *Bacchae* and *Iphigeneia at Aulis*. The ancient sources for Euripides' life and career are available (with translation) in D. Kovacs, *Euripidea* (Leiden, 1994) 3-141.

12. See P.T. Stevens, 'Euripides and the Athenians', *JHS* 76 (1956) 87-94 on Euripides' level of popularity in Athens.

13. See A.S. Owen (ed.) *Ion* (Oxford, 1939) xxxix-xli for the sort of historical concerns that traditionally influenced dating of the play: for example he mentions the Ionian Revolt of 412, which he argues *Ion* must have pre-dated because the tone of the play is not 'to win the Ionians back to their allegiance, but rather to make them proud of their present position'. Similarly, at line 1592, Rhium is mentioned, which Owen suggests may be a reference to Alcibiades' demonstration there in 419.

14. Zacharia (n. 7) 3-5.

15. I do not include *Rhesus*, which is usually thought to be the work of a fourth-century poet, while *Cyclops* is a satyr-play, and so stylistically different from tragedy.

16. *Ion* has a 27.9% resolution rate, compared with the 26.8% of *Trojan Women* (415) and the 34.8% of *Helen* (412). The resolution percentage shows a trend, rather than providing an accurate way to pinpoint plays, since not every single play fits the pattern perfectly (for example *Alcestis*, produced in 438, has a lower resolution rate than *Hippolytus* of 428). For this method of dating, see T.B.L. Webster, *The Tragedies of Euripides* (London, 1967) 1-9; M. Cropp and G. Fick, *Resolutions and Chronology in Euripides: the Fragmentary Tragedies* (London, 1985). For a more detailed account of its application to *Ion*, see Owen (n. 13) xxxvi-xxxvii; K.H. Lee (ed.) *Ion* (Warminster, 1997) 24-6.

17. J. Diggle's edition of the *Oxford Classical Text* of *Ion* puts the play at *c.* 413.

18. Csapo and Slater (n. 1) 221-38.

19. See Pickard-Cambridge (n. 1) 146 for the likely distribution of roles in *Ion*: the first two actors play Ion and Creousa, while the third actor plays Xouthos, the Priestess, and Athene, who are on-stage with the two main characters. Creousa's servant is probably also played by the third actor (though could be played by the actor who played Ion); Hermes must not be played by the actor who plays Ion, as it would not allow time for a costume change; the Messenger could be any actor but the one who plays Creousa.

20. The play's financial backer (*chorêgos*) was responsible for selecting the chorus, as well as providing training space and meals. Antiphon's *On the Choreut* 11-13 describes the process, and implies that selecting the best chorus without incurring any hostility was a time-consuming and delicate process. For the role of the *chorêgos*, see n. 3 above.

21. Choruses performed at a wide range of occasions, from private weddings and funerals to state-organised religious festivals. Like the tragic chorus, these choruses consisted of ordinary citizens, and choral participation was regarded as a sufficiently important part of civic training and education that Plato can describe the uneducated man as 'he who has not participated in a chorus' (*Laws* 654a). For further reading, see C.J. Herington, *Poetry into Drama: Early Tragedy and the Greek Poetic Tradition* (Berkeley, 1985) esp. 3-41; T.B.L. Webster, *The Greek Chorus* (London, 1970).

22. Aristotle, *Poetics* 1456a25-32 claims that irrelevant choral odes (*embolima*) were first introduced by the tragic poet Agathon. While older commentaries on Euripides plays sometimes dismiss odes as irrelevant if the connection is not obvious, more recent scholarship tends to demonstrate that these odes in fact have a thematic connection.

23. Poetic debates over the 'best thing' can be found in Sappho fr. 16 V, where the poet rejects the competing claims of cavalry and ships in favour of 'whatever one loves', and in Pindar's praise poetry, which discusses the relative merits of wealth and athletic excellence (e.g. *Olympian* 2.52-5; *Pythian* 2.56, 5.1-4; *Isthmian* 3.1-3). Pindar *Olympian* 1.1-11 ranks the relative merits of water, gold and the Olympic Games, each the best in their own category.

24. Divine prologues occur at Euripides' *Alcestis, Hippolytus, Trojan Women*, and *Bacchae*. Sophocles' *Ajax* also begins with a prologue shared by a god and a mortal.

25. See e.g. D.J. Conacher, 'The Paradox of Euripides' *Ion*', *TAPA* 90 (1959) 20-39 at 20-2; Lee (n. 16) 24-6.

3. Gods and Mortals

1. For anti-religious readings of the play, see G. Murray, *Euripides and his Age* (London, 1913); G. Norwood, *Essays on Euripidean Drama* (Berkeley, 1954); T.G. Rosenmeyer, *The Masks of Tragedy* (Austin, Texas, 1963) 105-52. For a pro-Apollo stance, see F.M. Wasserman, 'Divine Violence and Providence in Euripides' *Ion*', *TAPA* 71 (1940) 587-604; A.P. Burnett, 'Human Resistance and Divine Persuasion in Euripides' *Ion*', *CP* 57 (1962) 89-103.

2. Gods (or deified heroes) appear in Euripides' *Alcestis, Andromache, Bacchae, Electra, Helen, Heracles, Hippolytus, Ion, Iphigeneia Among the Taurians, Orestes, Suppliant Women, Trojan Women;* Sophocles' *Ajax, Philoctetes*; Aeschylus' *Eumenides* (not including *Prometheus Bound* as a work by Aeschylus).

3. See D. Mastronarde, 'The Gods', in J. Gregory (ed.) *A Companion to Greek Tragedy* (Oxford, 2005) 321-33 at 325-30 on the functions visible gods can have in tragedy.

4. Aristophanes *Women at the Thesmophoria* 450-2. In *Frogs*, Euripides is said to pray to 'other private gods' (888-93), and is called an 'enemy of the gods' by Aeschylus (836).

5. E.g. H.P. Foley, *Ritual Irony: Poetry and Sacrifice in Euripides* (Ithaca, 1985) 258; S. Goldhill, *Reading Greek Tragedy* (Cambridge, 1986) 234-5; A. Michelini, *Euripides and the Tragic Tradition* (Madison, 1987) 315-20.

6. Cf. M.R. Lefkowitz, ' "Impiety" and "Atheism" in Euripides' Dramas', *CQ* 39 (1) (1989) 70-82 (reprinted in J. Mossman (ed.) *Oxford Readings in Classical Studies: Euripides* (Oxford, 2003) 102-21), who argues for the essential traditionalism of Euripides' position, and suggests that the complaints among the human characters are a result of Euripides' 'realistic' style, rather than a change in the nature of divinity.

7. It is important to distinguish between literary portrayals of the gods, and how they are represented in more civic contexts such as cult or public oratory. See R. Parker, 'Gods Cruel and Kind: Tragic and Civic Theology', in C.B.R. Pelling (ed.) *Greek Tragedy and the Historian* (Oxford, 1997) 143-60 for an analysis of these differences.

8. The new intellectual movement in Athens is associated with thinkers such as Protagoras, Prodicus and Gorgias (known as the sophists). For an account of the sophistic movement, see W.K.C. Guthrie, *A History of Greek Philosophy* (Cambridge, 1969). For the influence of their ideas on Euripides, see D.J. Conacher, *Euripides and the Sophists: Some Dramatic Treatments of Philosophical Ideas* (London, 1998); W.R. Allan, 'Tragedy and the Early Greek Philosophical Tradition', in Gregory (n. 3) 71-82.

9. Socrates in *Clouds* is linked with Wrong Argument, and presented as a new-fangled intellectual whose teaching encourages disrespect for traditional values and for one's elders.

10. Socrates' trial was not purely a religious issue: an underlying motive was also his associations with the Spartan-imposed regime of the Thirty Tyrants which had recently been overthrown. Nevertheless, the overt charge was that of impiety, and Socrates' defence speech in Plato's *Apology* shows that this was taken seriously.

11. Cf. Lefkowitz (n. 6) who notes how characters expressing rationalistic or atheistic views turn out to be mistaken.

12. For the balance between divine will and chance in the play, see V. Giannopoulou, 'Divine Agency and Tyche in Euripides' *Ion*: Ambiguity and Shifting Perspectives', *ICS* 24 (1999) 257-71.

13. See also G. Gellie, 'Apollo in the *Ion*', *Ramus* 13 (2) (1984) 93-101, who argues that the light-hearted tone of the play precludes any serious criticism of Apollo.

14. Cf. S. Barlow, *The Imagery of Euripides* (London, 1971) 50: 'Apollo must be not only as Creousa sees him, but as Ion sees him and the chorus sees him. To take only one of these views as the truth is like believing Ophelia's mad scene contains the only real clue to Hamlet's character.'

15. Cf. I. Rutherford, 'Apollo in Ivy: the Tragic Paean', *Arion* 3 (1) (1995) 112-35 at 129-31. See also W.D. Furley, 'Hymns in Euripidean Tragedy', *ICS* 24-5 (1999) 183-97 at 188-9.

16. As D.J. Conacher, 'Some Profane Variations on a Tragic Theme', *Phoenix* 23 (1) (1969) 26-38 points out (and *pace* Burnett (n. 1)) Ion makes it clear in this passage that he objects to Apollo's rape as well as his alleged abandonment of the child. See also M. Lloyd, 'Divine and Human Action in Euripides' *Ion*', *A&A* 32 (1986) 33-45 at 36-7. A similar idea occurs at the start of *Bacchae*, where we are told that Semele's sisters refused to believe she was pregnant with Zeus' child, and assumed she was trying to cover up an affair with a mortal man (lines 26-30). Here too, the doubters turn out to be wrong – and are punished by Dionysus as a result (31-4).

17. Cf. J. Larue, 'Creusa's Monody: *Ion* 859-922', *TAPA* 94 (1963) 126-36; Furley (n. 16) 189-90; K. Zacharia, *Converging Truths:*

Euripides' Ion and the Athenian Quest for Self-Definition (Leiden, 2003) 90-2. K.H. Lee (ed.) *Ion* (Warminster, 1997) on 112-83 notes the structural and thematic similarities between Ion and Creousa's songs.

18. For example, Chryses' prayer to Apollo in *Iliad* 1.37-42, where the priest names the god's cult sites and titles as well as the previous aid he has given, before making his request. This pattern is also apparent in the *Homeric Hymns*: for example, the two *Hymns to Apollo* describe Apollo's birth on and connection with Delos and with Delphi; the *Hymn to Hermes* tells the story of how he acquired his powers and skills; the *Hymn to Demeter* explains how Demeter's cult at Eleusis came to exist.

19. The lyre usually symbolises Apollo's role as patron of the music and the Muses: the *Homeric Hymn to Hermes* tells the story of how Apollo acquired the lyre from Hermes, its inventor, while the *Homeric Hymn to Delian Apollo* describes the infant Apollo announcing his intention to play the lyre and shoot the bow (131-2). For Apollo as musician, see *Iliad* 1.603, 24.63; *Odyssey* 8.488. The lyre is also found as a symbol of civilisation and order: see P. Wilson, 'Athenian Strings', in P. Murray and P. Wilson, *Music and the Muses: the Culture of Mousike in the Classical Athenian City* (Oxford, 2004) 269-306.

20. Cf. Lloyd (n. 16) 36.

21. Ancient concepts of rape and sexual consent differed from ours. I use the term 'rape' throughout, but it should not be taken to suggest that the Greeks' concepts of sexual violence exactly overlap with ours. For a discussion of Greek thought on the subject, see T. Harrison, 'Herodotus and the Ancient Greek Idea of Rape', in S. Deacy and K.F. Pierce, *Rape in Antiquity* (London, 1997) 185-208.

22. Similarly, Poseidon's rape of Pitana and Apollo's rape of Evadne in Pindar, *Olympian* 6 are presented as a source of honour for the women and their descendants. See N. Loraux, *The Children of Athena* (Princeton, 1993) 189 for a contrast with *Ion*. We find the same idea elsewhere in heroic myth: for example in the *Iliad* we are told that Hermes seduces and impregnates a young girl called Polymele (16.179-92), but the pregnancy appears to have no negative effect on the girl's social status or subsequent marriageability. For rape in myth, see S. Deacy, 'The Vulnerability of Athena: Parthenoi and Rape in Greek Myth', in S. Deacy and K.F. Pierce, *Rape in Antiquity* (London, 1997) 43-63.

23. Both rape and adultery were serious crimes under Greek law, though adultery was considered worse because it implied willingness on the woman's part to cheat on her husband: cf. Lysias 1.32. See K.J. Dover, *Greek Popular Morality in the Time of Plato and Aristotle* (Oxford, 1974) 147.

4. Mothers and Children

1. Herodotus 1.30. Similarly, when Achilles in the *Iliad* makes a speech about the fragility of human fortune, using his father Peleus as a case-study, the fact that Peleus has only one child who is destined to die young is conceptualised as an evil great enough to balance out all the other good things the gods have given him (24.527-42).

2. Thus, scholars who seek to defend Apollo from criticism argue that he is not blamed for raping Creousa *per se*, but only for his subsequent abandonment of the child of this rape. See for example A.P. Burnett, 'Human Resistance and Divine Persuasion in Euripides' *Ion*', *CP* 57 (1962) 89-103 at 90-1. This line somewhat overstates the case, for as we shall see below the rape is also regarded as inappropriate irrespective of the child's fate. However, Burnett is right to note that the abandonment is consistently presented as the more serious crime.

3. E.g. F.I. Zeitlin, 'Mysteries of Identity and Designs of the Self in Euripides' *Ion*', *PCPS* 35 (1989) 144-97 (reprinted in F.I. Zeitlin, *Playing the Other* (Chicago, 1996) 285-338), N.S. Rabinowitz, 'Raped or Seduced? And Abandoned: Kreousa, Ion, Xouthos', in *Anxiety Veiled: Euripides and the Traffic in Women* (Ithaca, 1993) 189-222.

4. The Greeks tend to flag the socio-economic bond between child and parent rather more overtly than modern readers are used to, and use it to stand in for the nature of parenthood more generally. For example, in Euripides' *Medea*, Medea comments that killing her children will mean she is not economically provided for in her old age (1032-5), while in Euripides' *Trojan Women*, Hecuba laments her grandson Astyanax by noting that he will not now be able to keep his promise to provide her with a burial (1180-5). The fact that these pragmatic (and by modern standards rather selfish) concerns were used to represent the parent's emotional loss suggests that these aspects of parenthood were viewed as part of the more important kinship bond.

5. Cf. A.S. Owen (ed.) *Ion* (Oxford, 1939) on 237; F. Solmsen, *Electra and Orestes: Three Recognitions in Greek Tragedy* (Amsterdam, 1967) 40; K.H. Lee (ed.) *Ion* (Warminster, 1997) 186.

6. Cf. D.J. Conacher, 'The Paradox of Euripides' *Ion*', *TAPA* 90 (1959) 20-39 at 21.

7. Some scholars suggest that Ion takes Xouthos' attempts at physical contact to be a homosexual advance. See U. von Wilamowitz-Moellendorf, *Euripides: Ion* (Berlin, 1926) 111; B.M.W. Knox, *Word and Action: Essays on the Ancient Theater* (Baltimore, 1979) 260.

8. This change in tone would be still more marked if we followed the manuscript, where Ion exclaims *'ea'* ('aha!') upon realising Xouthos must know who his mother is (241); Diggle's OCT follows Bothe's emendation of *ea* to *ek*, rendering the line 'from what mother was I born to you?'.

9. The decision to accept the newborn child into the household was made on the tenth day of its life, and killing or causing the death of a baby before this time was acceptable. Plato *Theaetetus* 160c-161e describes the examination of a baby in conjunction with the formal decision over whether to raise it or not. See C. Patterson, ' "Not Worth the Rearing": The Causes of Infant Exposure in Ancient Greece', *TAPA* 115 (1974) 103-23 and R. Garland, *The Greek Way of Life: From Conception to Old Age* (London, 1990) 84-93 for the historical evidence for child-exposure.

10. Cf. A. Saxonhouse, 'Myths and the Origins of Cities: Reflections on the Autochthony Theme in Euripides' *Ion*', in J.B. Euben (ed.) *Greek Tragedy and Political Theory* (Berkeley, 1986) 252-73.

11. As H.P. Foley, *Female Acts in Greek Tragedy* (Princeton, 2001) 143-4 notes, mothers in tragedy are sometimes presented as unusually assertive when it comes to giving advice to their sons: in particular Aethra in Euripides *Suppliant Women* and Jocasta in *Phoenician Women*.

12. See R. Osborne, 'Law, the Democratic Citizen, and the Representation of Women in Classical Athens', *Past and Present* 155 (1997) 3-33 (reprinted in *Studies in Ancient Greek and Roman Society* (Cambridge, 2004) 38-60).

13. Cf. Demosthenes 57.20; Plutarch *Themistocles* 32.2.

14. Zeitlin (n. 3) 147.

15. For the bond between Achilles and Thetis, see *Iliad* 1.351-427; 16.221-4; 18.35-136; 24.126-40. For Hector and Hecuba, see 6.253-85; 22.79-89, 431-6; 24.208-17, 748-59.

16. The humour of *Women at the Thesmophoria*, however, relies on the idea that Euripides is posing a threat to women by *accurately* describing their activities, rather than unfairly portraying them in a negative light. In any case, using a comedy as evidence of ancient attitudes is highly problematic, because it is hard to interpret exactly how the comic distortion operates. Is portraying Euripides as a misogynist funny because it exaggerates something the Athenians felt to be true, or is it that it is such an absurd idea as to be funny?

17. See J. March, 'Euripides the Misogynist', in A. Powell (ed.) *Euripides, Women and Sexuality* (London, 1990) 32-75. C.B.R. Pelling, *Literary Texts and the Greek Historian* (London, 2000) 196-218 discusses the possible Athenian responses to powerful female figures in Euripidean drama.

18. For the social position of women, see J. Gould, 'Law, Custom and Myth: Aspects of the Social Position of Women in Classical Athens', *JHS* 100 (1980) 38-59 (reprinted in J. Gould, *Myth, Ritual, Exchange and Memory* (Oxford, 2001) 112-57).

19. Menander *The Girl with Cropped Hair* 435-6, cf. Lucian *Timon* 17. For childbirth rather than marriage as the final transition of female sexual maturity, see E. Cantarella, *Pandora's Daughters: The Role and Status of Women in Greek and Roman Antiquity* (Baltimore, 1987) 47; K. Dowden, *Death and the Maiden: Girls' Initiation Rites in Greek Mythology* (London, 1989) 43-4.

20. F.M. Dunn, 'The Battle of the Sexes in Euripides' *Ion*', *Ramus* 19 (2) (1990) 130-42 at 132-3 points out how unusual such a represen-tation of a rape in Greek tragedy is.

21. For tragic representations of women, see H. Foley, 'The Conception of Women in Athenian Drama', in H. Foley, *Reflections of Women in Antiquity* (Pennsylvania, 1981) 127-68; Foley, *Female Acts in Greek Tragedy* (n. 11) 201-42 on vengeful wives; F.I. Zeitlin, 'Playing the Other: Theater, Theatricality and the Feminine in Greek Drama', in J.J. Winkler and F.I. Zeitlin (ed.) *Nothing to do with Dionysos?* (Princeton, 1990) 63-96; J. Mossman, 'Women's Voices', in J. Gregory (ed.) *A Companion to Greek Tragedy* (Oxford, 2005) 352-66.

22. Cf. Foley, *Female Acts in Greek Tragedy* (n. 11) 125-6, 272.

23. For example in Sophocles' *Antigone*, Ismene agrees that Creon's action is wrong, but argues that as a woman it is not her place to subvert it (58-68). Similarly, in *Women of Trachis*, Deianeira's motiva-tions for taking action are entirely sympathetic, but her action nevertheless brings about disaster.

24. We find a similar motif at *Medea* 410-45, where the Chorus describe Medea's proposed vengeance as overturning the established system and revealing the hypocrisy of men. As in *Ion*, the Chorus of *Medea* is portrayed as having a close and supportive relationship with the main female character, and this bond is founded on their shared femaleness.

25. See for example Rabinowitz (n. 3) 14; V. Wohl, *Intimate Commerce: Exchange, Gender, and Subjectivity in Greek Tragedy* (Austin, 1998) 179, 182; Foley, *Female Acts* (n. 11) 12-13.

26. Zeitlin, 'Playing the Other' (n. 21) 68-9.

27. *Iphigeneia at Aulis; Trojan Women.* Other examples include the threat to Andromache's second child in Euripides' *Andromache*, the denial of marriage to Antigone in Sophocles' *Antigone* and to Electra in his *Electra*.

5. Identity and Empire

1. The *genethlia* was celebrated shortly after the child's birth, and is described by Plato at *Theaetetus* 160e. See W.K. Lacey, *The Family in Classical Greece* (London, 1968) 111-12; R. Garland, *The Greek Way of Life: From Conception to Old Age* (London, 1990) 93-6.

2. A. van Gennep, *The Rites of Passage* (London, 1960).

3. See L.B. Carter, *The Quiet Athenian* (Oxford, 1986) 52-75 on the anti-democratic connotations of the noble youth who rejects political participation.

4. See R. Mitchell-Boyask, 'Euripides' Hippolytus and the Trials of Manhood (the Ephebia?)', in M.W. Padilla (ed.) *Rites of Passage in Ancient Greece* (Lewisburg, Pa., 1999), 42-66 on Hippolytus. N.S. Rabinowitz, 'Raped or Seduced? And Abandoned: Kreousa, Ion, Xouthos', in *Anxiety Veiled: Euripides and the Traffic in Women* (Ithaca, 1993) 189-222, notes the parallel between the two plays.

5. Sappho frr. 107 and 114 V are wedding songs expressing the bride's reluctance. M. Alexiou, *The Ritual Lament in Greek Tradition* (Cambridge, 1974) 120 notes that the motif continues into modern Greek song.

6. S.E. Hoffer, 'Violence, Culture and the Workings of Ideology in Euripides' *Ion*', *CA* 15 (2) (1996) 289-318 at 316-17 argues that the fairy-tale ending does not hide the real-life political complications, and that we are led to realise that Ion will face strife in Athens. However, Athene's speech surely goes a long way towards relieving this in the audience's minds, for we know Ion's rule in Athens is divinely ordained, and thus inevitable.

7. For the history of the autochthony myth in Athens (and particularly its representations in art), see H.A. Shapiro, 'Autochthony and the Visual Arts in Fifth-Century Athens', in D.A. Boedeker and K.A. Raaflaub (ed.) *Democracy, Empire and the Arts in Fifth-Century Athens* (Cambridge, Mass., 1998) 127-51.

8. For the functions of autochthony myths, see N. Loraux, *The Children of Athena* (Princeton, 1993) 37-71; A. Saxonhouse, 'Myths and the Origins of Cities: Reflections on the Autochthony Theme in Euripides' *Ion*', in J.B. Euben (ed.) *Greek Tragedy and Political Theory* (Berkeley, 1986) 252-73.

9. While the children of Heracles and the Dorians were initially two separate groups, they gradually became merged into one: cf. J. Hall, *Ethnic Identity in Greek Antiquity* (Cambridge, 1997) 60.

10. E.g. Thucydides 1.12.3, 3.92; Herodotus 1.56.

11. E.g. Herodotus 1.143 claims that the Ionians were ashamed to use their name, while Thucydides describes Spartan generals urging on their troops by reminding them of their natural military superiority to Ionians (5.9.1 and 7.5.4). Athenaeus 12.524f-526d collects a list of sayings about the Ionians. For Greek ethnic attitudes, see J. Alty, 'Dorians and Ionians', *JHS* 102 (1982) 1-14.

12. Part of the reason for the assimilation of the myth of the Dorians to the return of the children of Heracles to their native land may have been a desire to represent the Dorians as autochthonous too, and thus legitimise the invasion. See W. Allan, (ed.) *The Children of Heracles* (Warminster, 2001) 22-5.

13. Athenian autochthony is frequently found in patriotic rhetoric: for example Herodotus 7.161.3; Isocrates 4.24; Thucydides 2.36.1; Lysias 2.17.

14. F.I. Zeitlin, 'Mysteries of Identity and Designs of the Self in Euripides' *Ion*', *PCPS* 35 (1989) 144-97 (reprinted in F.I. Zeitlin, *Playing the Other* (Chicago, 1996) 285-338). D.J. Mastronarde, 'Iconography and Imagery in Euripides' *Ion*', *California Studies in Classical Antiquity* (1975) 163-76 (reprinted in J. Mossman (ed.) *Oxford Readings in Classical Studies: Euripides* (Oxford, 2003) 295-308) notes the way the imagery of autochthony runs throughout the play and underpins the dramatic action.

15. E.g. Saxonhouse (n. 8) 258-9; Zeitlin (n. 14) 171-2; Loraux (n. 8) 216.

16. See T. Gantz, *Early Greek Myth: a Guide to Literary and Artistic Sources* (Baltimore, 1993) 77-8 for the ancient sources for this story.

17. For example, in the *Iliad*, Athene takes off her female clothing and puts on Zeus' masculine tunic in order to take part in the fighting

(5.736, 8.387), and she participates more directly in battle than any other goddess (cf., for example, her role in guiding the *aristeia* of Diomedes in Books 5 and 6).

18. Cf. K. Zacharia, *Converging Truths: Euripides' Ion and the Athenian Quest for Self-Definition* (Leiden, 2003) 62; Loraux (n. 8) 8.

19. The Gigantomachy was indeed represented on the west pediment of Apollo's temple at Delphi. V.J. Rosivach, 'Earthborns and Olympians: the Parodos of the *Ion*', *CQ* 27 (2) (1977) 284-94 analyses the Chorus' description of the temple sculptures, and links it to the play's broader themes.

20. Cf. B. Goff, 'Euripides' *Ion* 1132-1165: the Tent', *PCPS* 34 (1988) 42-54. A.P. Burnett, 'Human Resistance and Divine Persuasion in Euripides' *Ion*', *CP* 57 (1962) 89-103 sees in the two drops the two opposing features of Creousa's character: the extremes of hatred and love she is capable of (98).

21. Goff (n. 20). See also Mastronarde (n. 14) who discusses this strand of imagery in *Ion*.

22. Cf. K.H. Lee (ed.) *Ion* (Warminster, 1997) on 224.

23. Loraux (n. 8) 201.

24. Cf. M. Lloyd, 'Divine and Human Action in Euripides' *Ion*', *A&A* 32 (1986) 33-45 at 44-5.

25. Hall (n. 9) 54-5 suggests that the stress on the foundation of Ionia by Athens operates as a method for denying Athens' Ionian heritage and emphasising her autochthony. Zacharia (n. 18) 45-6, however, argues that the end of the play alludes to Athens' Ionian ancestry as well as her future colonisation of the region.

26. Shared Ionian identity was a significant factor (or at any rate pretext) for the Athenians' assuming leadership of the Delian League, cf. Thucydides 1.95.1; see pp. 26-7 above.

27. Thucydides' pessimism about the Athenian empire may not be representative of general attitudes within Athens: cf. G.E.M. de Ste Croix, 'The Character of the Athenian Empire', *Historia* 3 (1954) 1-41. If modern scholars do tend to overstate the level of anxiety that the average Athenian would have felt about the empire, *Ion* could instead be read as a sign of the Athenians' essential confidence in the rightness of their rule.

28. E.g. Thucydides 1.38, where Corinth berates her colony Corcyra for disloyal behaviour. Strikingly, the Corcyraeans' defence (1.34) is that Corinth had failed to fulfil her obligations as a mother-city, thus implicitly conceding that under normal circumstances their rebellion would have been wrong.

29. Loraux (n. 8) 202-3 notes that the two words are in fact used interchangeably by Attic writers.

30. See for example D.J. Conacher, 'The Paradox of Euripides' *Ion*', *TAPA* 90 (1959) 20-39, who repeatedly uses the term 'propagandic' to describe any pro-Athenian speech in the play, and thus is led to defend the play from the charge of propaganda, by concluding that the critical elements in the characterisation of Apollo preclude *Ion* from being 'primarily a nationalistic, propagandic, play' (34-5). Similarly, G.B. Walsh, 'The Rhetoric of Birthright and Race in Euripides' *Ion*', *Hermes* 106 (1978) 301-15, recognises that the negative as well as the positive sides of national identity are explored in the play, so concludes that the play undermines the positive aspects of autochthony. Yet to see the bad aspects as wholly contaminating the good ones is just as one-sided as to regard the play as naively patriotic.

31. Loraux (n. 8) 209-10.

32. Tragedy's relationship to the ideology of the Athenian *polis* more generally is a subject of intense scholarly debate. For recent contributions, see J. Griffin, 'The Social Function of Attic Tragedy', *CQ* 48 (1) (1998) 39-61; R. Seaford, 'The Social Function of Attic Tragedy: a Response to Jasper Griffin', *CQ* 50 (1) (2000) 30-44; P.J. Rhodes, 'Nothing to do with Democracy: Athenian Drama and the Polis', *JHS* 123 (2003) 104-19; D. Carter, 'Was Attic Tragedy Democratic?', *Polis* 21 (2004) 1-25.

33. See K.J. Dover, *Greek Popular Morality in the Time of Plato and Aristotle* (Oxford, 1974) 301-6 on ancient views about individual patriotism.

34. Cf. E. Hall, 'The Sociology of Athenian Tragedy', in P.E. Easterling, *The Cambridge Companion to Greek Tragedy* (Cambridge, 1997) 93-126 at 100-3. Neither Aegeus nor Theseus is an unsympathetic character, but neither is a role-model for ideal behaviour. Aegeus is arguably depicted as foolish and easily duped, while Theseus is over-hasty and quick to condemn his son unfairly.

6. Happy Endings?

1. See M. Wright, *Euripides' Escape-Tragedies* (Oxford, 2005) 7-9 on the history of these terms and the associated scholarship.

2. Menander's *The Girl from Samos* turns around who are the father and mother of a newborn baby; *The Girl with Cropped Hair* is the story of twins abandoned at birth and recognised by tokens; *The*

Sicyonian contains a hero and heroine who both need to be identified as free-born Athenians in order to marry. See N. Zagagi, *The Comedy of Menander* (Bloomington and Indianapolis, 1995) 23-6 for the recognition story-pattern in Menander's work.

3. Cf. W.R. Allan (ed.) *Euripides: Helen* (Cambridge, 2008) 68-9.

4. These lighter tragic plots are not limited to Euripides: the fragments of Sophocles' *Tyro* plays are just as 'tragicomic' as any of Euripides' plays. See G. Moodie, 'Sophocles' Tyro and Late Euripidean Tragedy', in A.H. Sommerstein, *Shards from Kolonos: Studies in Sophoclean Fragments* (Bari, 2003) 117-38.

5. See R. Oswald, 'Exposure, myths and legends of', in *Brill's New Pauly*, Antiquity volumes ed. Hubert Cancik and Helmuth Schneider (Brill, 2007).

6. Cf. Apollodorus *The Library* 1.4-5; Callimachus *Hymn to Zeus* 49; Strabo *Geography* 8.7.5.

7. See K. Zacharia, *Converging Truths: Euripides' Ion and the Athenian Quest for Self-Definition* (Leiden, 2003) 150-5, who argues that *Ion* should be considered a tragedy.

8. Cf. H.D.F. Kitto, *Greek Tragedy: a Literary Study* (2nd edn London, 1950) 327-47; B.M.W. Knox, *Word and Action: Essays on the Ancient Theater* (Baltimore, 1979) 257-70; G. Gellie, 'Apollo in the *Ion*', *Ramus* 13 (2) (1984) 93-101.

9. Aristotle *Poetics* 1449a14-15. See Allan (n. 3) 67-8 for a discussion of Aristotle's impact on later definitions of tragedy.

10. The non-select plays (also called alphabetical plays) are: *Electra; Helen; Heracles; Children of Heracles; Suppliant Women; Ion; Iphigeneia at Aulis; Iphigeneia Among the Taurians; Cyclops.*

11. The select plays are *Alcestis; Andromache; Bacchae; Hecuba; Hippolytus; Medea; Orestes; Phoenician Women; Trojan Women.*

12. Allan (n. 3) 69.

13. E.g. N. Loraux, *The Children of Athena* (Princeton, 1993) 209-10; W.G. Arnott, 'Realism in the *Ion*', in M.S. Silk, *Tragedy and the Tragic* (Oxford, 1996) 110-18 at 110-11; N.S. Rabinowitz, 'Raped or Seduced? And Abandoned: Kreousa, Ion, Xouthos', in *Anxiety Veiled: Euripides and the Traffic in Women* (Ithaca, 1993) 189-222 at 219-22.

14. Cf. K.H. Lee (ed.) *Ion* (Warminster, 1997) on 1549-1622: '[Apollo's non-appearance] must leave the audience pondering the cost of the grand plan which invests the Ionian race with the superiority of an immortal ancestor.'

15. See K.J. Dover, *Greek Popular Morality in the Time of Plato and Aristotle* (Oxford, 1974) 147.

16. Cf. K.F. Pierce, 'The Portrayal of Rape in New Comedy' in S. Deacy and K.F. Pierce (eds) *Rape in Antiquity* (London, 1997) 163-84; R. Omitowoju, *Rape and the Politics of Consent in Classical Athens* (Cambridge, 2002) 169-82.

17. Cf. K.H. Lee, 'Shifts of Mood and Concepts of Time in Euripides' *Ion*', in M.S. Silk, *Tragedy and the Tragic* (Oxford, 1996) 85-118 at 95: 'Xouthos' simple-minded and shallow attitudes ensure that we treat him principally as a legal necessity in Apollo's ordering of the future. We should waste no time wondering about his future.' See also A.S. Owen (ed.) *Ion* (Oxford, 1939) xxx; Knox (n. 8) 267.

18. Plato *Republic* 377e-391e attacks poetry for representing gods and heroes in a negative light, and argues that appropriate poetry will represent the gods as wholly beneficent, and heroes as better than ordinary men.

19. Cf. e.g. Loraux (n. 13) 209-10, as quoted in the previous chapter.

Guide to Further Reading

This is not intended to be a full bibliography on *Ion*, but a guide to the more accessible or stimulating material on the play and its contexts. For discussion of specific points, see the items referred to in the notes.

Abbreviations

A&A = *Antike und Abendland*
AJA = *American Journal of Archaeology*
CP = *Classical Philology*
CQ = *Classical Quarterly*
CR = *Classical Review*
ICS = *Illinois Classical Studies*
JHS = *Journal of Hellenic Studies*
M-L = Meiggs, R. and Lewis, D.M., *A Selection of Greek Historical Inscriptions to the end of the Fifth Century B.C.* (revised edn, Oxford, 1989)
PCPS = *Proceedings of the Cambridge Philological Society*
TAPA = *Transactions of the American Philological Association*

Commentaries on *Ion*

Lee, K.H. (ed.) *Euripides'* Ion (Warminster, 1997).
Owen, A.S. (ed.) *Euripides'* Ion (Oxford, 1939).

Translations

Davie, J. *Euripides: Heracles and Other Plays*, with introduction and notes by R.B. Rutherford (London, 2002).
Di Piero, W.S., *Ion: Euripides*, with introduction, notes and commentary by P. Burian (New York, 1996).

Grene, D. and Lattimore, R. (eds) *The Complete Greek Tragedies: Euripides IV* (Chicago, 1958).

Kovacs, D. *Euripides: Volume IV* (Cambridge, Mass. 1999).

Waterfield, R. *Euripides: Orestes and Other Plays*, with introduction by E. Hall and notes by J. Morwood (Oxford, 2001).

Introductions to Greek Tragedy

Easterling, P.E. (ed.) *The Cambridge Companion to Greek Tragedy* (Cambridge, 1997). A collection of essays on various aspects of tragedy, including historical contexts and modern reception.

Gregory, J. (ed.) *The Blackwell Companion to Greek Tragedy* (Oxford, 2005). Similar to the above: introductory essays on a wide range of topics.

Books and articles about *Ion*

Burnett, A.P. 'Human Resistance and Divine Persuasion in Euripides' *Ion*', *CP* 57 (1962) 89-103.

Conacher, D.J. 'The Paradox of Euripides' *Ion*', *TAPA* 90 (1959) 20-39.

Larue, J. 'Creusa's Monody: *Ion* 859-922', *TAPA* 94 (1963) 126-36.

Lloyd, M. 'Divine and Human Action in Euripides' *Ion*', *A&A* 32 (1886) 33-45.

Loraux, N. 'Kreousa the Autochthon: a Study of Euripides' *Ion*' in J.J. Winkler and F.I. Zeitlin (eds) *Nothing to Do with Dionysos?* (Princeton, 1990) 168-206.

Mastronarde, D.J. 'Iconography and Imagery in Euripides' *Ion*', *California Studies in Classical Antiquity* 8 (1975) 163-76, reprinted in J. Mossman (ed.) *Oxford Readings in Classical Studies: Euripides* (Oxford, 2003) 295-308.

Zacharia, K. *Converging Truths: Euripides'* Ion *and the Athenian Quest for Self-Definition* (Leiden, 2003).

Zeitlin, F.I. 'Mysteries of Identity and Designs of the Self in Euripides' *Ion*', *PCPS* 35 (1989) 144-97, reprinted in F.I. Zeitlin, *Playing the Other* (Chicago, 1996) 285-338.

Contexts of tragedy

Csapo, E. and Slater, W.J. (eds), *The Contexts of Ancient Drama* (Ann Arbour, 1995). Excellent source-book for our understanding of ancient drama, containing translations of the Greek and Roman documentary evidence.

Pickard-Cambridge, A.W. *The Dramatic Festivals of Athens*, 2nd edn, revised by J. Gould and D.M. Lewis (Oxford, 1968). A thorough discussion of the evidence for the ancient festival-contexts. Not for beginners.

Reception of ancient drama

Burian, P. 'Tragedy Adapted for Stages and Screens: the Renaissance to the Present', in P.E. Easterling (ed.) *The Cambridge Companion to Greek Tragedy* (Cambridge, 1997) 228-83.

Hall, E. and Macintosh, F. *Greek Tragedy and the British Theatre, 1660-1914* (Oxford, 2005).

Macintosh, F. 'Tragedy in Performance: Nineteenth- and Twentieth-Century Productions', in P.E. Easterling (ed.) *The Cambridge Companion to Greek Tragedy* (Cambridge, 1997) 284-323.

Glossary

Technical terms

Agôn: a formal debate-scene between two characters.

Chorêgos: person in charge of funding the dramatic production (allocated to a rich citizen as part of the Athenian *leitourgia* (taxation of the wealthy) system).

Choreut: individual chorus member.

Deus ex machina: literally 'god from the crane': a divine appearance, where the god appears elevated above the stage, to speak to the mortal characters. This device often occurs at the end of Euripidean tragedies.

Episode: sections of spoken dialogue between actors (rather like scenes in a modern play).

Exodos: final section of the play, between the last choral ode and the end.

Kommos: lyric interchange between actors and chorus.

Mêchanê: crane used to hoist actors up for divine appearances.

Monody: solo song by an actor.

Oikos: home, family unit.

Paian (plural **paianes**): a religious song in honour of Apollo.

Parodos: song sung by the chorus as they enter the theatre.

Polis: Greek city-state.

Protagonist: first actor in a troupe, who played the most important roles.

Stasimon (plural **stasima**): choral ode divided into metrically equivalent stanzas (strophe and antistrophe). Choral odes without this metrical pattern are not called stasima.

Stichomythia: alternating lines of dialogue between two characters.

Metrical terms

Greek metre is built out of 'short' (marked as ∪) and 'long' (marked as –) syllables. Sometimes the metre may allow the poet to choose either a long or a short syllable (in which case the sign ∪̲ is used).

Glossary

Specific metres

Anapaests: lyric metre: often used for the choral *parodos* because it evokes a marching rhythm. The basic rhythm is ∪ ∪ –

Iambics: metre used for the spoken sections of tragedy (more precisely iambic trimeters). The basic rhythm is ∪̲ – ∪ –

Trochaics: the basic unit of this metre is an iambic one backwards: i.e. – ∪ – ∪̲

Metrical terms in general

Astrophic: lyric written in free metre rather than divided into strophes (stanzas).

Lyric: the metres used for sung sections of tragedy (both choral and solo), which tend to be complex and variable.

Resolution: the name for when a long unit is swapped for two short ones, which are considered to be equivalent. This can happen at any point in the line, and can affect one or both of the long units. Thus, a 'resolved' iambic might take the form ∪ ∪ ∪ ∪ – , or alternatively ∪ ∪ ∪ ∪ ∪ ∪ in place of the rhythm given above; in the first case the first long has been resolved into two shorts; in the second case both longs have been resolved.

Chronology

Historical events	Literary events
	501 City Dionysia re-organised: beginning of contest records
c. 507 Reforms of Cleisthenes (beginning of democracy at Athens)	
490 Battle of Marathon	
	487 First performance of comedy at the City Dionysia (tragedy has been performed at the festival since possibly 534)
	484 First victory of Aeschylus
481-79 Defeat of second wave of Persian invasion (battles of Salamis and Platea)	**c. 480** Birth of Euripides
	468 First victory of Sophocles
462 Reforms of Ephialtes (radicalisation of democracy at Athens)	**c. 460** Thucydides born
	455 First production by Euripides
451 Pericles' Citizenship Decree	
	449 Competition for the best tragic actor initiated
	441 First victory of Euripides (plays unknown)
	c. 445-426 Herodotus active
	438 *Alcestis*
431 Beginning of Peloponnesian War	**431** *Medea*
430 Plague at Athens	**c. 430-28** *Children of Heracles*
	428 *Hippolytus*
427 Gorgias arrives in Athens (start of the sophistic movement)	**c. 425** *Andromache*
	c. 424 *Hecuba*
	c. 424-20 *Suppliant Women*

Historical events	Literary events
421 Peace of Nicias (war between Athens and Sparta stops)	
	c. 422-16 *Electra, Heracles*
416 Athenian destruction of Melos	
415 Sicilian Expedition (defeated in 413).	**415** *Trojan Women*
	c. 415-13 Probable date of *Ion*
	412 *Helen*
	c. 412 *Cyclops* (satyr play)
411 Oligarchic revolutions in Athens (democracy restored again in 410)	**411** Aristophanes' *Women at the Thesmophoria*
	c. 409 *Phoenician Women*
	407/6 Death of Euripides in Macedon
	406/5 Death of Sophocles
	after 406: *Bacchae* and *Iphigeneia in Aulis* win first prize posthumously
404 Defeat of Athens – end of Peloponnesian War	**405** Aristophanes' *Frogs* presents Euripides and Aeschylus competing in the underworld for the throne of tragedy
399 Trial and execution of Socrates	

Index

actors, 10, 30-1
adulthood, transition to, 9, 69-71
Aeschylus, 37, 92; *Libation Bearers*, 16, 90; *Eumenides*, 59, 75-6, 83, 90
agôn scenes, 32-3
Apollo, felt to be immoral, 18-19, 36, 41, 44-6, 50; defences of, 36, 41, 46, 47-8; as Ion's father, 17, 43, 46-7, 51, 52-3, 56, 64, 96; as rapist, 10, 19, 48, 64; criticised by Ion, 11, 37, 41, 43-4, 47; failure to appear at end, 34, 49, 94, 97; *see also* gods
Aristophanes, 88, 91, 93; *Assembly-Women*, 61; *Clouds*, 39; *Frogs*, 25, 98-9; *Women at the Thesmophoria*, 38, 62
Aristotle, 18, 92-3, 98
Athene, 11, 15, 34, 35, 49, 72, 74, 75-6, 77, 78, 79, 80, 95, 97; *see also deus ex machina*
Athens, in fifth century, 26-7, 29, 70, 79-80; in tragedy, 82-3; in *Ion*, 18, 35, 41, 69, 71-85, 93; *see also* autochthony; Ion, nationality of; ideology, civic
autochthony, 73-8, 84

Cecrops, 76-7

children, importance of, 12, 32, 51, 62; *see also* parenting
Chorus, in general, 10, 30, 31-2; in *Ion*, 11, 12, 13, 14, 30, 31-2, 65-6, 71, 75, 76, 81, 90, 98
citizenship decree, 60
colonies, 80; *see also* empire
Comedy, Old, 87, 88, 91; New, 87-90; *see also* Aristophanes; Menander
comic elements in *Ion*, 12, 49-50, 55, 59, 61, 75, 86, 90, 97-8
contexts of drama, 24-6
Creousa, as rape-victim, 41, 44, 48, 64, 83-4, 94, 96; as a mother, 9, 52, 54, 56, 58-61, 96; as a wife, 32, 62-4, 67-8; as an Athenian, 72, 74, 77, 78; attitude to Apollo, 13, 16, 37, 41, 44-6, 50, 96-7, 99; vengeance of, 13, 14, 34, 51, 52, 63, 64-5, 70, 72, 78; complicity with Chorus, 13, 30, 32, 65-6, 71, 98

dating of *Ion*, 28-30
Delian League, 26
Delphi, 10, 11, 35, 40, 42, 45, 70
Demetrius, 18
deus ex machina, 15-16, 32, 33, 34-5
Dionysia, 24-6, 28, 80, 82

125

EURIPIDES: ION
Laura Swift

Euripides' *Ion* is the story of a young man's
search for his identity, and a woman's attempt
to come to terms with her past. Through the
story of a divine rape and its consequences,
it asks questions about the justice of the gods
and the nature of parenthood, encouraging its
audience to consider contemporary concerns
through the filter of traditional myth.

This detailed study outlines the pre-history
and later reception of the Ion myth, and
provides a literary interpretation of the play's
main themes, aiming to combine analysis of
the text with a consideration of its cultural
contexts. Chapters on religion, family, and
national identity investigate how Euripides
handles these issues in the light of the values
of his day, and a chapter on genre discusses
the play's upbeat ending and explores how we
should define tragedy.

Laura Swift is Junior Research Fellow in
Classics, Trinity College, Oxford.

Cover illustration: Detail of an Athenian red-figure cup:
Cecrops (left) and Athene (right) taking Erichthonius
from Ge (centre). Antikensammlung, Staatliche Museen
zu Berlin, no. F2537.

Duckworth
90-93 Cowcross Street
London EC1M 6BF
www.ducknet.co.uk

**DUCKWORTH
COMPANIONS
TO GREEK AND
ROMAN TRAGEDY**

Series editor:
Thomas Harrison
University of Liverpool

This new series provides
accessible introductions
to ancient tragedies. Each
volume discusses the main
themes of a play and the
central developments in
modern criticism, while
also addressing the play's
historical context and the
history of its performance
and adaptation. A guide to
further reading, glossary and
chronology are included, all
Greek and Latin is translated,
and technical and theoretical
terms are clearly explained.

ISBN 978-0-7156-3744-9

9 780715 637449